MAGNETIC

JOE CALLOWAY

MAGNETIC

THE ART OF
ATTRACTING BUSINESS

WILEY

This book is dedicated to
Ellen Bush, Bob Calloway, and John Calloway.
Family is everything.

Contents

1

Why Magnetic Matters

This is what magnetic looks like. This is the art of attracting business.

I took this photo from my car one wet, dreary morning outside the Pancake Pantry in Nashville, Tennessee. This photo perfectly captures the core message of this book and what it means to your business: To be so good at what you do that your customers tell others, creating a steady stream of new customers.

The ideal caption for this photo would be a statement from W. Edwards Deming, who many people believe was the greatest business thinker of our time:

"Profit in business comes from repeat customers, customers that boast about your product or service, and that bring friends with them."

For a business . . . any business . . . your business . . . that's the gold standard. Magnetic means that the customers come to you. Customers are drawn to you.

The Art of Attracting Business

So, how do you make it happen? The quick answer is that you become incredibly good at what you do. So good that people talk about it. For the Pancake Pantry it's a combination of a great location combined with really good pancakes served by really good people at a fair price. That's it. It's simple, but don't kid yourself that it's easy. It's not. There's no one-size-fits-all template that this or any other book can slap on top of your business to make it successful.

On the one hand, what it takes to make a business magnetic is so simple that it'll make you slap your forehead and think "I *knew* that!" On the other hand, there are a thousand ways to do it and you have to figure out which ways match up with who you are as a business, your culture, your business model, your strengths, your weaknesses, your competitive advantages and disadvantages, your personality and the personalities of those you work with, your values, your vision, your mission—it's all part of the mix that is distinctly you as a business leader, your colleagues or employees as a team, and all of it together as a business.

Every business is different. We're different in every way imaginable.

Every business is the same. We all want and need customers.

Ideas That Work across the Board

We're going to take a look at magnetic businesses, people, and organizations of all kinds, and see what is truly effective for them in attracting new customers. One of the things I love most about these ideas is that they can help attract business to a huge corporation, a mom and pop business, a law practice, a dance studio, a baseball team, a retail store, a nonprofit organization, a franchise, a consultant, a hospital, or any other kind of business endeavor. These ideas work across the board, and they can work for you.

You're going to discover how people and businesses that are magnetic are making it happen on a consistent basis. You will have light bulbs exploding in your mind as you spot the ideas that feel like a perfect fit for you. It's all good stuff, believe me, but there will be particular ideas and strategies throughout the book that will have you thinking, "That would definitely work for me," "I can easily adapt that idea to what I do," and "I can do that beginning right now."

I have helped nonprofit organizations adapt ideas from manufacturing companies to help them attract more donors. I have worked with banks to adapt strategies from successful hospitals to help them attract more customers. Your best idea is *over there*. I'm going to show you some of them. Then you take over the creative part and adapt it to what you do to help you to become magnetic.

What's Not in the Book

This book focuses on one thing above all others: creating the experiences that spark the positive word of mouth that will drive new business to you. It is about the attitudes, strategies, and tactics that make that happen.

This book is about what customers say about you. It's not about what *you* say about you. That's another book and, in fact, there are countless books about marketing, advertising, websites, and what you should say on social media. That's all part of the mix, and posting, tweeting, and linking online with customers is fine, but it's not the focus of this book.

This book is about what matters most—the stories that your customers tell about you, not the stories that you tell about yourself. Your priority should be the experiences you create that cause your customers to, as Deming said, "boast about your product or services."

It's not just important. It's the *most* important factor in your business success. This is about what the marketplace tells us is happening.

Here's a sprinkling of the data (more follows in later chapters):

1. 85 percent of fans of brands on Facebook recommend brands to others. (Syncapse)
2. 43 percent of consumers are more likely to buy a new product when learning about it through word of mouth on social media. (Nielsen)

3. 77 percent of consumers are more likely to buy a new product when learning about it through word of mouth from friends or family. (Nielsen)
4. 81 percent of U.S. online consumers' purchase decisions are influenced by their friends' social media posts. (Market Force)

It IS Your Marketing

Becoming magnetic is a way of thinking about your business so that the work you do, the products you make, and the service you deliver to your customers are no longer separate from your marketing. They *are* your marketing.

Please take special note of the statistic above: 81 percent of U.S. online consumers' purchase decisions are influenced by their friends' social media posts. Not what the *business* says on social media, but what customers say *about the business* on social media. That's the point that so many people in business miss. They spend too much time and thought on what they post on social media, and not nearly enough on improving performance that will positively affect what their customers post *about them* on social media.

We'll take a lot of different approaches and look at a lot of different perspectives on what it takes to become magnetic. We'll look at companies, businesses, people, and organizations that are seemingly completely unlike you or your business. But they will offer lessons in being magnetic that you can adapt and use immediately to attract business.

Where We're Going

At the end of each of the following chapters, you will find questions meant to provoke thought and action about the ideas in the book. The questions are designed to be useful if you simply ask them just of yourself, but you'll see that they use the pronoun "we" to encourage discussions with your team.

Remember where we're going with all of this. We're going to look at what magnetic companies do, which you can do, to attract business. Remember that the key is what your customers say about you to others. You will create the experiences for them that will drive positive word of mouth, which is the most powerful magnet for business ever known.

Let's go.

2

The Power of Word of Mouth

The Greatest Marketing Program of All Time

Here's one more restaurant story with a lesson that has everything to do with your business, no matter what it might be. My family went to Maui on vacation. My longtime friend, fellow foodie, and fine restaurant enthusiast Kris Young told me that while on Maui, we absolutely had to go to Mama's Fish House.

Another good friend and aficionado of great restaurants, John Bledsoe, told me, "Mama's Fish House may be the most beautiful setting of any restaurant that I know of, and I'm not really even a Hawaii person."

So I asked the rest of the world what they thought of Mama's. I went on the Internet. Here's what the rest of the world told me:

- 3,104 reviews on Yelp averaging 4.5 stars out of 5.
- 5,981 reviews on TripAdvisor.com averaging 4.5 stars out of 5.
- Named second most popular restaurant in the United States by Open Table.
- Named one of the Top 10 Fine Dining restaurants in the United States by Trip Advisor.

I defy you to show me any advertising, selling, or marketing program as powerful as the overwhelmingly positive word of mouth that Mama's Fish House has going for it. It is, quite simply, the greatest marketing program of all time.

What Mama's Means to You

So we went to Mama's Fish House. I've been to great restaurants all over the world, and I will tell you without reservation that Mama's is as good as it gets. Period. I invite you to go online yourself and read what people say about it (including my own reviews). It may be the most amazing example of positive word of mouth I have ever seen. It is what drives tens of thousands of customers there to spend an insane amount of money (it's very expensive).

But the lesson of Mama's Fish House and what it means to you requires a clear understanding of how it works. All of that positive word of mouth driving all of those customers and all of that revenue to Mama's comes from three things:

1. A breathtaking setting on the Maui beach in the single most charming restaurant I've ever seen.
2. A truly wonderful staff, from the valet who parks your car to the hostess, the waitress, and every single person working there whom we interacted with. They were absolutely great.
3. The food. This is at the center of the Mama's word of mouth miracle: food like you've never tasted before. It darn near defies description.

And that's the lesson for all of us: The product *is* the marketing. That's the punch line. That's the silver bullet. That's the "secret of success" that everyone's looking for. To all of the people over the years who have said to me some version of "I just need something that will drive more customers to me," I say this:

Do great work.
Make a better product.
Give better service.

This is what will drive more customers to you. There is absolutely no force or power on planet Earth that will create more customers for a business than to have people like my friend Kris saying things like "you absolutely have to go there" to potential customers like me.

The Most Important Factor

The single most important factor in the future success of your business is this: what your customers tell people about their experience with you. What this means to you is that creating positive experiences for your customers is the single most important thing that you can do to grow your business.

Lest you think I'm overstating things or exaggerating the importance of customer word of mouth to your business, your future, and your ultimate success or failure, let me be excruciatingly clear: Nothing—absolutely nothing—affects the success of your business more than customer word of mouth. Reputation has always had a greater impact on purchase decisions than any other factor, and today, because of the Internet, the power of customer word of mouth is far, far greater than ever before. In the future, it will become even more powerful.

Customer recommendations, whether your customers are retail consumers or business to business, are your greatest driver of growth. Customer recommendations give you the magnetic power to attract business.

If statistics make your eyes glaze over, then you can skip this next section. But here's what I want you to understand down to your bones: If your business isn't focused on driving positive word of mouth, then the train is leaving the station without you. This is where your market is going. This is where your customers and potential customers are going. Your business will live or die, thrive or struggle, based on your ability to harness the power of your customers to drive new customers to you.

It's true whether you are a high-tech startup, a bar, law firm, hospital, nonprofit charitable organization, bank, consulting firm, or a retail store in the mall or on the Internet. The power of positive word of mouth isn't an "interesting" idea. This is how you will succeed and then sustain and grow your success.

For those who like numbers to go along with the blindingly obvious, here are some statistics on the effect of positive word of mouth as compiled by customer referral management company Ambassador:

84 percent of consumers say they either completely or some-what trust recommendations from family and friends about products—making these recommendations the information source ranked highest for trustworthiness. (Nielson)

74 percent of consumers identify word of mouth as a key influencer in their purchasing decision. (Ogilvy/Google/TNS)

68 percent trust online opinions from other consumers. (Nielson)

88 percent of people have their reasons for trusting online reviews written by other consumers as much as they trust recommendations from personal contacts. (BrightLocal)

72 percent say reading positive customer reviews increases their trust in a business. (BrightLocal)

On social media, 58 percent of consumers actively share their positive experiences with a company and ask family and friends for their opinions on brands. (SDL)

Word of mouth has been shown to improve marketing effec-tiveness by up to 54 percent. (MarketShare)

84 percent of consumers reported always or sometimes taking action based on personal recommendations. 70 percent said they did the same of online consumer opinions. (Nielson)

43 percent of social media users report buying a product after sharing or favoriting it on Facebook, Twitter, or Pinterest. Over half of purchases inspired by social media sharing occur within one week of sharing or favoriting, and 80 percent of purchases resulting from social media shares occur within three weeks of sharing. (VisionCritical)

Millennials ranked word of mouth as the #1 influencer in their purchasing decisions about clothes, packaged goods, big-ticket items (like travel and electronics), and financial products. Baby Boomers also ranked word of mouth first as the marketing influencer in their purchasing decisions about big-ticket items and financial products, and ranked it as the third-highest influencer on their decisions to buy packaged goods. (RetailGlobal)

77 percent of brand conversations on social media are people looking for advice, information, or help. (Mention)

Whom Do You Ask?

In your own experience, when you are considering making a purchase, an investment, even a donation to a charitable organization, where do you go for information, guidance, and advice? Whom do you ask?

Used to be we'd ask our personal friends, our family, or our coworkers. Now, in addition to those trusted sources, we ask everybody. The way we do that is by asking the Internet.

Think about your most recent trip to the Internet to visit Yelp, TripAdvisor, Angie's List, Google Reviews, Yahoo Local Listings, City Search, Consumer Search, the Better Business Bureau, or any of the countless review and evaluation sites. In addition to those, there are industry- and profession-focused sites on which customers or members exchange information about who is doing good work and who isn't. There's the mother of all "find it on the Internet" sites: Google. And finally, there are all of the social media sites like Facebook, Instagram, Twitter, LinkedIn, and dozens more where conversations about whom to do business with take place 24/7.

Deciding to Buy (or Not to Buy)

When is the last time you made an online search for recommendations, reviews, or information? For most people the answer will certainly be within the past week. For many it will be within the past 24 hours.

You go online to search for ratings, reviews, opinions, and comments about whomever or whatever company you are considering doing business with, and generally speaking, you make your decision pretty quickly. This is especially true if the reviews and ratings tend to trend heavily in one direction or the other.

If you are considering, for example, joining a fitness club and the Yelp ratings for the club you're looking at average one star out of five, then your decision is made in that very moment. That fitness club has been declared "loser" in the eyes of its customers (or former customers), therefore it is automatically eliminated from further consideration.

The same holds true for businesses that have extremely positive word of mouth and recommendations. The higher the ratings and the more there are of them, the more likely you are to give them your business. They're magnetic, and they pull you and your money straight to them.

People in the market for a new car used to rely on the car salesman to guide their buying decision. We would listen carefully to what the salesperson told us about which brand or model was the best buy. No more. Now we may not even feel a need to talk with the salespeople at all.

Remember that we're talking about the same word of mouth that has always driven purchase decisions. But now with the reach of the Internet, your satisfied customers don't tell four or five people; they potentially tell thousands. Of course, the same holds true for dissatisfied customers. Today they can keep countless potential customers from choosing you.

What this means is that your existing customers must be a vitally important part of your sales and marketing strategy.

Zero Moment of Truth

Pardot, a Salesforce company, explains the new buzz phrase in marketing, the "zero moment of truth (ZMOT)." ZMOT refers to the point in the buying cycle when the consumer researches a product, often before the seller even knows that they exist. The number of consumers researching a product online prior to purchase has been on the rise in recent years as the Internet and mobile devices continue to advance. In 2011, the average shopper used 10.4 sources of information before making a purchase decision, compared with half as many sources in 2010.

A Google/Shopper Sciences Marco Research study a few years ago revealed that:

50 percent of consumers used a search engine to get information;
49 percent of consumers talked with family or friends about potential purchases;
38 percent of consumers comparison-shopped online;
36 percent of consumers sought information from a brand/manufacturer website;
31 percent of consumers read product reviews or endorsements online;
22 percent of consumers sought information from a retailer/store website;
22 percent of consumers read comments following an article/opinion piece online;
18 percent of consumers became a friend, a follower, or "liked" a brand.

Bear in mind that these numbers, while the most recent available, become obsolete almost immediately, and they continue to rise dramatically. Think of yourself as the best market research on this. The vast majority of people reading this book can nod their heads right now in acknowledgment of the fact that they and everyone they know make buying decisions in this new "outside influenced" way.

It's Not Just Retail Consumers. It's B2B.

A lot of my clients are like me in that their marketplace is business to business (B2B). Your customers are companies and the people in those companies who make buying decisions. Just like my customers, your customers are making their decisions on whom to business with based on what other customers tell them. The trend of B2B buying decisions being influenced by word of mouth is more than just growing. It's a veritable market reality tidal wave.

Studies show that today's B2B buyers have done more than two-thirds of their decision-making research before they make contact with a potential vendor; 75 percent start the process with an online search; and 76 percent leverage relationships with people they know personally or professionally to get advice on where to take their business.

91 percent of B2B buyers are influenced by word of mouth when making their decision to buy. (USM)

61 percent of IT buyers report that colleague recommendations are the most important factor when making a buying decision. (B to B Magazine)

56 percent of B2B purchasers look to offline word of mouth as a source of information and advice, and this number jumps

to 88 percent when online word of mouth sources are included. (BaseOne)

These are high-value customers because referral customers have the highest retention rate, purchase more over time, and in turn become a source of additional referrals.

Smart companies in the B2B arena no longer use their websites just as platforms from which they can tell the world how great they are at what they do. Instead, they feature their customers' testimonials and positive stories about their experiences with the company.

I live in the B2B world and I know that my business will live or die, prosper or wither based on what my clients say about me to one another and to others who are considering doing business with me. My opportunity is to do great work, make my clients happy, and help them achieve their goals. In doing this, I create the stories that they tell about me and assure that they drive new business my way.

The Most Significant Shift

In the future, the power of customers to tell the world about their experiences with your business, good or bad, will only grow. This may well cause the most significant, fundamental shift in how we do business since the advent of the Internet.

As buyers continue to value customer feedback over advertising, marketing materials, self-promotion on websites, and what have been, up until now, other "normal" ways of attracting new business, customer feedback will have a growing impact on advertising and marketing strategies.

Remember, it's no longer what you say about you that matters most to buyers. It's what your customers say about you.

Rethinking Your Strategy

While monitoring and participating in social media to engage with customers is obviously important, don't make the fundamental mistake of overestimating its place in the food chain of attracting new customers and keeping the ones you've already got happy and loyal.

Many businesses waste an amazing amount of time and effort wondering which social media platform is best for them. Should we focus on Twitter? Instagram? Will we all be on Vine with six-second videos? How often should we post, and what should our posts say?

Of course you want to have a savvy and effective social media strategy, but let's please not take our eye off the ball. The source of future growth for your business will increasingly be found in what customers say about you. Put your thought, time, and talents to work making your customers happy. Then let *them* carry the message of your value to the marketplace.

- What company, product, or service do I recommend to others?
- What are our customers saying about us?
- Are they actively recommending us?
- What steps can we take to find out what our customers are saying about us and to stay current with that information?
- Do we encourage our customers to recommend us?
- What are people saying about our competition?

3

The Hard Work of Making It Simple

Get Your Thinking Clean Enough

Steve Jobs once said that it takes a lot of hard work to get your thinking clean enough to make things simple. He was right. It's much easier to make things more complicated than it is to simplify.

The ultimate purpose of strategy is to create an intense focus on the few things that matter most. If you are willing to create an intense focus throughout your organization on what matters most, then your chances of success increase greatly.

The strategies presented in the next two chapters, The Three Things You Want Them to Say and The Three Things You Must Get Right, are powerful and effective in large part because of their simplicity. There's no question that the strategies work. They've been proven to work over and over again by businesses large and small, professional practices, nonprofits, and organizations of every kind and description.

For them to work, however, you must be willing to do that hard work to get your thinking clean enough to simplify how you think about your business.

You must clarify.

You must focus.

Everyone on the team must buy in and be committed.

You must execute with consistency.

Do that, and you become magnetic. Your customers will drive a steady stream of new business to you.

- Are we willing to do the hard work necessary to make things simple?
- If not, let's say so and keep things complicated, slower than they need to be, and generally ineffective.

(*continued*)

(*continued*)

- If we are willing to do that hard work, are we committed to clarify, focus, and execute with consistency from this moment on?
- If so, prepare to succeed beyond what you have imagined.

4

The Three Things You Want Them to Say

"You Should Try This Website Designer, Doctor, Book, Accountant, and Computer."

- I mentioned to a couple of my colleagues that I was in the market for a new website designer. They both recommended Brian Kraker. I hired him and he's great. I have since recommended him to others who have hired him.
- My doctor, Dr. Lee Fentriss, was recommended to me by my sister. Lee has now been my doctor for over 10 years.
- The last book I bought was recommended to me by my friend, Mark Sanborn.
- My accountant, James Weinberg, was recommended to me over 25 years ago. He's still my accountant.
- The reason I use a Mac laptop is because years ago I asked a group of business associates their opinion on the PC vs. Mac question. They overwhelmingly recommended Mac. The rest is history—I've been a Mac guy ever since.

A huge number of the products you buy, the services you buy, and the people you do business with were recommended to you by friends, family, or by total strangers on the Internet.

What your customers say about you is the most powerful magnetic force you can possibly have working in your favor. So don't leave it to chance. Be in control of it.

"Go ahead, ask the Internet. I'll wait."

One company that totally "gets it" about the power of customer word of mouth is HTC. In a recent television commercial, the British actor Gary Oldman is in an office holding up a smartphone. Looking into the camera, he says, "I could tell you how amazing the all new HTC One is, but I won't. Because let's face it, you either already know, or you want to see what others have to say about it. So go ahead, ask the Internet. I'll wait."

When people ask you about your business and you can say "Ask the Internet," that's an incredibly powerful competitive position to hold.

Whom Do You Recommend?

I asked a few of my friends to tell me whom they regularly recommend to others and why. Here's what they said:

- Adam Palmer: Spotify. "It allows you to seamlessly aggregate, share, and listen to music."
- Rose Mary Winget: Uline. "They answer my call before it rings and already have all of my customer information pulled up."
- David Earnhardt: Emma. "They have given us an easy-to-use, affordable, and powerful marketing tool to share and promote our filmmaking services."
- Jane Devou: JP's Restaurant. "Their exceptional staff, fabulous menu, and inviting atmosphere create an experience!"
- Barry Owen: Dixie Door, Inc. "They do one thing: garage doors—and they do it well and efficiently at a surprisingly fair price."

By the way, my own garage door opener (Liftmaster) has performed amazingly well for 12 years. I'm thinking that it is surely due to run out of steam someday soon. Because Barry recommends Dixie Door so enthusiastically and had such a great customer experience, I'm calling them when the time comes to replace my Liftmaster garage door opener. Great performance for existing customers like Barry Owen creates positive word of mouth for Dixie Door. That positive word of mouth creates new customers like me for Dixie Door.

Please note that none of my friends talked about anything particularly unusual or out of the ordinary that their recommended company does. What all of those companies have in common is that they do ordinary things extraordinarily well. It's about making something easy to do (Spotify); quick response and knowing the customer (Uline); being easy to use, affordable, and effective (Emma); people, product, and atmosphere (JP's Restaurant); and efficiency and a fair price (Dixie Door).

Everyone Gets It

I work with hundreds of business owners and managers each year, and when we talk about the power of word of mouth and how it is the key to attracting business and driving growth, everyone "gets it." Everyone understands and accepts the idea that positive word of mouth is the key factor in their future success.

Beyond that, though, the thought process seems to be "I know how important positive word of mouth is, and I sure hope our customers are saying great things about us." They go back to work with a firm resolve to encourage everyone on the team to do a really great job and get that customer recommendation machine working for them.

Which, of course, is useless. "Do a really great job" means nothing. You've got to get specific. You've got to be intentional.

Are You Intentional?

Giving lip service to the strategy of customer-driven growth is as useless as giving lip service to the idea of "continuous improvement" or "exceeding our customers' expectations." In most businesses, ideas like that are simply slogans and posters on the break room walls, not a reality.

We have to get beyond just the *idea* of customer-driven growth and get to the strategic and tactical reality of it. We have to be intentional about making it happen. To be intentional means that everything is driven with the purpose of creating happy, satisfied customers who recommend you to your target market. For some, this approach just isn't complicated enough. They think that for a strategy to be effective, it should have hundreds of moving parts. In reality, just the opposite is true.

At their annual senior leadership meeting, the CEO of one of my client companies said, "The price we pay for making things too complicated is immeasurable. It slows us down, makes for bad decisions, and scatters our efforts." Almost everyone agrees with that idea. Complication is generally ineffective. Simplicity gets it done.

What Do We Want Our Customers to Say about Us?

Consider the logic and strength behind this incredibly simple approach to your business: What do we want our customers to say about us?

The key to this idea working is to not settle for something like "we want them to say good things." That's meaningless. They key is to be focused and specific on *exactly* what you want your customers saying about you. This is the starting point for being a truly magnetic business.

You will need to give this some serious thought and discussion. First, you identify the specific things your customers say that will indicate extreme satisfaction with your business and will drive new business to you through the power of positive word of mouth. Let's call them our "what we want them to say" statements. Then you focus the attention and efforts of your entire business on creating the customer experiences that result in those statements. The end result is that you have satisfied, loyal customers who become your never-ending source of new business.

In case you're wondering why I suggest that you should choose three ideal customer statements, it's simply because the number three is so effective. We can wrap our heads around three things. Fourteen things? A lot tougher to think about. You can certainly go with one, two, four, or five things, but I recommend three.

Make An Emotional Connection

No matter what kind of business you are in, to be truly magnetic you have to make an emotional connection. If you sell light bulbs on the Internet for industrial use, your goal should be to have all of your customers saying "I love these guys." The emotional connection comes from how they feel when they do business with you.

It goes beyond the rational connection you might make with price, quality, and value.

The Journal of Marketing Research reports that research by Keller Fay Group found that brands that inspire a higher emotional intensity experience three times as much word of mouth activity as less emotionally connected brands. That same study also found that highly differentiated brands have greater word of mouth.

There's an accounting firm in Nashville, Tennessee, whose entire marketing effort is built around customer testimonials in which they all say "I Love My CPA!" Love is the ultimate and most powerful magnetism in business. Love is pure emotion, and to get to the point where your customers love you and tell others about it, you simply have to make that emotional connection.

To drive significant positive word of mouth, you can't just do a good job. You have to be so good at what you do that it inspires your customers to talk about you. The companies that get the greatest amount of word of mouth are found at both ends of the performance spectrum—the positive end and the negative end.

Those companies that do an extraordinary job inspire positive comments, and that magnetic force brings additional customers to them. The ones that are perceived as doing a poor job inspire negative comments, terrible reviews, and one-star ratings both online and in person. More and more, this kind of negative word of mouth will cause potential customers to immediately eliminate you from consideration.

Don't Overthink It

As you think through what you want your customers saying about you and the word of mouth buzz that you want to create, please don't overthink it. What are three rock solid statements about you that, if heard over and over again from lots of people by potential customers, would be likely to drive them to you like steel balls to a powerful magnet?

Keep it focused on those core things that attract your customers to you and keep them loyal. It can help to think in terms of what you really don't want your customers saying about you.

A few years ago, I was approached by a firm that does marketing for people who speak professionally. They wanted to build a marketing campaign for me that would have "everyone saying you're a rock star in the speaking business." I told them that very few, if any, of my satisfied clients use the words "rock star" to describe me, and that it's really not a description that I wanted to cultivate.

Neither do I want to be known for "lowest fee," "trendy programs," "really unusual thank you gifts," "will negotiate anything you want," "loves to work overseas," or any number of other things. Knowing what I *don't* particularly want my customers to say about me helps me get clarity on what I need to do well in order to get them to say the things that I *do* want them to say. More about that in the next chapter.

Your Three "What We Want Them to Say" Statements

Come up with three "what we want them to say" statements that you want from your customers. These can be different for everyone, as they depend on a multitude of factors including:

- the nature of your product or service;
- your competitive strengths (i.e. price, service, customization, the ability of your people to make positive connections with customers, your particular processes, the ease of doing work with you, etc.);
- where your customers will be making their recommendations. For the Nashville CPA firm, it's on their own website and in their advertising. For your business, it may be on TripAdvisor, Google Search, or on your Facebook page.
- the kind of customers and new business you want to attract. If you are priced higher than your competition, you certainly don't want to identify "they've got the lowest price" as one of your ideal "What We Want Them To Say" statements. You might, however, want to target "they're the best value."

In my *Magnetic: The Art of Attracting Business* keynotes and workshops, I give participants a list of possible "what we want them to say" statements to get them thinking about what would work for them, their business, and their growth strategy.

It's a take-home exercise, because to make it really work requires some thought and most likely input and discussion from your team. This list serves as a starting point for you to consider further, and I encourage people to come up with their own wording for "what we want them to say" statements.

The exercise is to choose three of these statements that you want your customers saying about you. Remember, you are free to come up with your own. These are just meant to get the thought process going:

- They always make me feel welcome.
- They respect and value my time.
- Their quality is the best.
- They are extremely responsive.
- I always feel like I'm important to them.
- Their service is the best.
- All of their people are great.
- Doing business with them makes me happy.
- They take care of me.
- I love doing business with them.
- They get it right every time.
- They make it very easy to do business with them.
- They have the best products.
- I trust them.
- They help me achieve my goals.
- I highly recommend them.
- They have the best prices.
- It doesn't matter whom you deal with—all of their people are great.
- They understand me/my business.
- It's a pleasure doing business with them.
- They always keep me informed.
- They really listen to me.
- They are problem solvers.

- They respect me.
- They give me the best value.
- I have absolute confidence in their work.
- They always do it when they say they will.

Once you've got your target "what we want them to say" statements, then you go to work to get the buzz started and keep it going. In the next chapter, we talk about what we do to make your "what we want them to say" statements become real and how to create the stories that you want your customers to tell about you.

- What do we want our customers to talk about?
  - Our product?
  - Our service?
  - Our people?
  - Our customization?
  - Our prices?
  - How easy we are to do business with?
- What do we NOT want our customers to say about us?
- Where do we anticipate that our customers' conversations about us will take place (i.e., face to face, on review sites, etc.)?
- What kind of new customers do we want our existing customers to drive to us?
- What are three rock solid statements about you that, if heard over and over again from lots of people by potential customers, would be likely to attract them to you like steel balls to a powerful magnet?
- From the list at the end of the chapter, which "what we want them to say" statements feel right to us? Why? What other statements might work better?

5

The Three Things You Must Get Right

A Simple, Powerful Formula to Attract Business

If I had to choose only one chapter of this book for you to read, this would be it. This is the core idea, the heartbeat, the absolute foundation of how to become magnetic. I'm going to give you a simple, powerful formula to attract business. It's been proven effective time and time again by every size and kind of business you can imagine. Part of the reason for its effectiveness is its simplicity. You can put this strategy to work for you immediately.

In the previous chapter, The Three Things We Want Them to Say, you began to think through and identify the three things that you want your customers to say about you. They are the "what we want them to say" statements. These are, in effect, the stories they will tell about their experiences with you. This is what reinforces their loyalty and attracts new customers to you. This is the power of positive word of mouth.

Now you'll identify the three things you must get right every time in order to drive those "what we want them to say" statements.

You may have a business with a thousand moving parts. You may feel, justifiably, that it's very complicated. But I assure you that if you simplify your thinking to get clarity on and focus on the three things you must get right every single day, it will be the guiding force that drives success.

This is where you put words into their mouths.

Wouldn't it be great if you could just put words into your customers' mouths? If you could create the content of the stories that they tell to others? The reality is that, in fact, you do create the stories your customers tell. You do it with every contact, at any point, between any customer or prospect and anyone on your team or anything about your company, from your advertising to your website.

The experiences you create, good, bad, or anywhere in between, are the stories that get told at all of those places where customers go to decide who to do business with. They go to friends, family, and coworkers. Believe me, and believe the research, when I tell you that they are going to the Internet in droves.

Here's the key idea, and it's what should be behind your strategy, your tactics, and every business decision you make:

Your existing customers should be driving a never-ending stream of new customers and new revenue to your business.

If they're not, then you're missing the point, you're missing the boat, and you're missing the greatest opportunity to grow your business. So how do you make it happen? You do it by getting three things right every time.

That's what you have to find out.

In a movie that a few of you may be old enough to remember, *City Slickers*, the character Mitch, played by Billy Crystal, learns the secret of life from Curly, played by Jack Palance. Curly tells Mitch that it's all about one thing. When Mitch asks what that one thing is, Curly simply tells him that that's what he's got to find out.

The secret to creating and sustaining a magnetic business that attracts a steady stream of customers is much the same. The difference is that the "magic" number for business is three. In business after business, I've seen that having three things to focus on and get right every time works so well for every kind of business.

I can't tell you what your three things are. Like Curly said, "That's what you have to find out." What I can do is give you a variety of examples of businesses that use the "three things" approach in different ways to drive their success. Your three will be determined by the "what we want them to say" statements and your own strengths and differentiators.

Solid Gold Strategy

I've got about as simple a business as anyone can have. My job is to help clients improve performance and grow their businesses. I do that through ideas presented in books and articles, advisory services to business leaders, and presentations and workshops at corporate meetings and events. I have no retail business except for the individuals who buy my books. I am squarely in the B2B marketplace.

It is with a great sense of gratitude that I can say that my business has been very successful. The reason for that success is that I've stayed focused on my own three things that I must get right. For over 30 years, this strategy has been solid gold for me.

Here are the three things I must get right every time:

1. Do great quality work for each client, and always be improving the quality of that work.
2. Be incredibly easy to work with.
3. Have an immediate response to customers, potential customers, and business partners.

That's it. These three things that I must get right have been the guiding elements of my business and how I spend every working day of my life for over 30 years. I have always been open to changing any or all of these three things, but so far there's never been the need to do so. I owe my success and, more important, my ability to sustain that success to these three things.

The first, doing great quality work for each client and always improving the quality of my work is, without question, my great overriding priority. Many people in my line of work spend most of their time in sales and marketing activities. My approach is that the work I do for clients is my most powerful sales and marketing activity, so that's where I put my effort.

Great work is magnetic. Nothing creates positive word of mouth better than doing a great job for your customers. That's where I place my bet. That's where I'm all in. Do great work and customers will come to me like steel balls to a magnet.

The second, be incredibly easy to work with, has been the ultimate tiebreaker for me. Lots of people tell me that their competition isn't very good. Wow. What's it like to live in that world? My competition is extremely good at what they do. I need tiebreakers, and being incredibly easy to work with is the one that fits me, my personality, and my strengths. I try to adhere to the philosophy espoused by my friend John DiJulius, who says, "The answer is yes. Now, what's your question?"

Finally, having an immediate response to customers, potential customers, and business partners is my personal "silver bullet" in business. Read more about this great business practice in the chapter "The Amazing, Simple, Overlooked Advantage."

The Grand Guarantee

In the book *Never By Chance—Aligning People and Strategy through Intentional Leadership*, which I cowrote with Chuck Feltz and Kris Young, we featured Western Water Works Supply Company, Inc. (WWWSC), a remarkable business located in central California. WWWSC is a distributor of materials and products that build and sustain America's waterworks infrastructure.

The company's vision and mission statement is: "We provide Smooth-Running Jobs from Start to Finish through our People, Products, and Systems to the premier underground contractors and water utilities." At the heart of that statement is their dedication to the idea of "smooth-running jobs."

The WWWSC website makes great use of testimonials from their customers, both written and on video. They are a prime example of a magnetic business powered by what their customers say about them. Here are a few examples of customer statements about WWWSC:

"WWWSC is very detail oriented in their quotes—and that's huge."

"They guarantee on time delivery, that the parts will meet spec, and that they will match the quote. What that means to me is that Western's committed to raising the bar on customer service."

"They believe in providing proper materials on time and I can vouch for that."

"They understand our business and that transcends to smooth running jobs."

"That orders going to be there when they say it's going to be there."

"We get a competitive product that's delivered on time."

You can see a pattern of three basic ideas coming through in these and many other testimonials:

- Their orders meet the specs of the job.
- They are very accurate in in matching the quote.
- They deliver on time.

The Grand Guarantee is where the three things that WWWSC must get right drive these very powerful testimonials, which, in turn, drive new business to WWWSC.

1. Accurate Orders: You get what you ordered, and it meets the specifications for the job.
2. Accurate Billings: Your invoice will match your quote.

3. Accurate Delivery Times: Your order will be delivered when we've agreed it will arrive.

WWWSC promises that if they make a mistake in any one of these areas, they will pay members of their Grand Guarantee Club $1,000.

They also measure their results in all three areas, track them internally and report them to the members of the Grand Guarantee Club every month. They also report the results on their website.

Bruce Himes, president of WWWSC, says, "When we deliver on those three things, our customers have a better chance of having a smooth-running job."

Do you see the alignment through all of this?

The core of their vision and mission is to make sure that their customers have a smooth-running job.

For their customers the three things that make up a smooth-running job are orders that meet the specs, accurate invoices, and on-time delivery.

The three things they must always get right, which they guarantee with $1,000 when they miss the mark, are accurate orders, accurate billings, and accurate delivery times.

That Won't Work in My Business

The one thing that almost every business I work with says is some version of, "Now Joe, you have to understand that our business is very different." Okay. And you have to understand that the fundamental way to win customers, keep them, and have them drive new customers to you is pretty much the same for every business, including yours.

There are people who, no matter what proven ideas they are given, cling to "but that won't work in my business" as their excuse for being stuck smack in the middle of mediocrity. Another favorite is "but that's too simple to work." That one truly makes me want to beat my head against a brick wall. It's the simple ideas and strategies that almost always work. "Complicated" makes for bad, ineffective strategies. Simple gets it done.

Let's take what most would consider a unique business and see if the "three things you must get right" has any practical application.

Business Case Study: A Magnetic and Feared Hollywood Reporter

Nikki Finke is one of the most successful Hollywood reporters ever. She was a journalist for a number of newspapers, joining the *Los Angeles Times* covering entertainment, She subsequently became West Coast editor for *The New York Observer* and then wrote Hollywood business columns for *New York* magazine. From 2002 until 2009 she wrote her "Deadline Hollywood" column for *LA Weekly*.

Finke had a distinctive approach to her reporting, to say the least. *The New York Times* described her as "in your face," "feared by Hollywood executives," and a "Hollywood power broker." In 2007, Finke won the Los Angeles Press Club's Southern California Journalism Award for "Entertainment Journalist of the Year" with the judges commenting: "Reading Nikki Finke's salaciously candid coverage of Hollywood and its inhabitants almost feels like a guilty pleasure. She mixes the news with fearless finger-wagging that's just fun to read no matter the subject. She tackles the industry monoliths without the kiddy gloves and she seems to have command of the beat."

Finke has launched a website dedicated to fictional short stories and novellas on the entertainment industry. She will charge her followers (she has well over 250,000 of them on twitter) from \$1 to \$3 to read these.

So what in the world does the business (and, yes, it's most definitely a business) of being a feared Hollywood writer have to do with the idea of success through three things you must get right? Simply this: *The New York Times* (Business section) says that Nikki Finke has three things that are, to her, "the words I live by:"

1. You're best when angry.
2. Write what you really know.
3. Tell the truth about Hollywood.

Do it Your Way

Again, the key is having clarity on your three things and living by them.

In terms of having an effective "three things you must get right" strategy, I would suggest that Nikki Finke isn't that much different from the successful trucking freight line that lives by:

1. Pick it up when you said you would.
2. Deliver it when you said you would.
3. Deliver it intact and all there.

Or the restaurant franchise that has the entire team focused on:

1. Serve the food fast and hot.
2. Deliver exceptional value.
3. Be the friendliest place our customers go.

You might have a different set of three things you must get right for your restaurant. They could be:

1. Use only the freshest, highest-quality ingredients.
2. Make each order one at a time with care and love.
3. Find out each customer's name and use it when you say thank you.

This is the best part, that you do this in the way that works for you, your business, and your business model. But it's also the part that trips some people up. They want someone to tell them what to do. They want a formula or template or the three easy-to-follow steps.

The templates and formulas don't exist! There simply is no one-size-fits-all solution, and the exciting business reality is that you have to figure it out for yourself. What works for Walmart won't work for Target. In-N-Out Burger has different strengths, values, and strategies than Five Guys Burgers and Fries.

I am often asked to speak to association meetings of professional speakers. I also do coaching and advisory work with speakers. One thing I always make very clear is that the way I do it isn't the way they should do it. They can get ideas from me and even take and adapt what I do to their own business. But trying to simply lay someone else's formula for success over your unique business is usually a recipe for failure. I tell them that if anyone ever says "I've got a guaranteed system that will work for you" to keep their money in their pockets, turn, and run. There's no such thing.

Success in business requires research, discovery, and a degree of creativity in finding out everything from your purpose and values to what kind of people you want to hire to what you want your customers to say about you to the three things you must get right. It's your business. You have to make it work.

If you read what seems to be the current line of thinking among business gurus, you will often see them decry the fallacy of "best practices." I get that and agree with it in terms of tactics.

But the cliché "success leaves clues" is a cliché for a reason—
there's great truth in it. When you look at successful, magnetic
companies, there are qualities and similarities of a "best practices"
mind-set that come into play.

The Good News: You Have Control

The truth is that you likely won't succeed if you try to copy the
specific tactics that work for someone else. But what is also true
is that most companies that are effective magnets for new
business all have some version of "the three things you must
get right." It's not their strategies or tactics that are the same. That
wouldn't make sense. Every business has its own particular
strengths, employee talent mix, market challenges and opportu-
nities, etc.

What these powerful magnet companies have in common
is this: They each figure out the small handful of things that
they must do to create satisfied customers. Then they bring the
focus of the entire organization onto those few things. Here's the
flip side of that equation: If you can't tell me the three most
important things in your business, then how do you know what
to work on every day? How do you know what your priorities
are? How do the people on your team know what matters most?

I can assure you with absolute confidence that if you
understand the three things that are most important to your
customers and then focus everyone and everything on delivering
those three things every time, you will experience remarkable
success.

The stories that your customers tell about you drive the
buying decisions of your potential customers. To not have
control over those stories would be a very scary thing. The
good news is that, in fact, you do have control over those stories.

There's one question for you, and it may be one of the most important questions you can answer:

- What are the three things we must get right every time?

6

The Best Idea Ever

Make Sure the Other Guy Wins

In 1978 I attended a weekend seminar on selling and negotiating at the Red Lion Inn near Sea-Tac Airport in Seattle, Washington. I had just entered the real estate business and was looking for ideas to give me a competitive edge. The seminar had a number of different instructors and sessions on various aspects of selling and negotiation, but one presentation that focused on one particular idea not only stuck with me, but became the basis for how I would do business throughout my entire career.

It's been decades since that weekend seminar, and the idea that I learned has been creating magnetism in my life ever since. When I share it with my clients and audiences, I tell them that it is the single most powerful and effective idea I know. It is, quite simply, the best idea ever.

The idea is to make sure the other guy wins. It's the win–win strategy.

An Elegant Equation to Explain Everything

In the movie *The Theory of Everything,* British theoretical physicist and cosmologist Stephen Hawking is portrayed as being on a relentless search to find one simple, elegant equation to explain everything. That's pretty much what the win–win strategy is for me.

Certainly in my business, but also in my personal relation-ships, with my family, and with the world in general, I have found that the win–win strategy has never failed me. That's a very bold statement, but I make it very intentionally. For me, it's a bulletproof strategy. It's always worked.

Most people's initial reaction to the win–win strategy is that it can't work because if the other guy wins, then they must lose. They believe that life is a zero-sum game in which there are winners and losers and that they must be one or the other. There are certainly a few situations in which that's the case. It's true in checkers, arm wrestling, chess, and any number of other competitive games. In order for you to win, the other guy or team has to lose.

But in real life—in the world in which you and I do business, have friendships, raise families, and do almost everything that we do—the "I win/you lose" dynamic not only isn't applicable, it's nonsense. In the real world, very rarely does it makes sense for you to make someone else lose. In fact, when you create losers, it almost always ends up working against you.

This isn't about being "nice," and it most certainly isn't about being a wimp or a pushover. On the contrary, this is about being smart enough, creative enough, and strong enough to create transactions and relationships in which you create winners. It's not necessarily easy, but it's always worth the effort.

Look at the Options

Let's consider what the options are in transactional relationships:

- **I Lose–You Lose.** This really is starting at the bottom of the list with the least desirable option of all. This is the situation in which either both parties make really dumb deals in which neither of them gets what they want, or one or both parties are so snarky that the strategy is "If I can't get what I want then neither will you." This would be a situation in which you sabotage or deliberately destroy a potential opportunity because you feel like the other side is winning more. You're willing to take a loss to keep them from getting a win. However you look at it, though, you're still taking a loss. Perennial victims, really incompetent businesspeople, and complete dopes are fans of this strategy. They are known for alienating customers and for destroying organizations from the inside out.

- **I Lose–You Win.** Just minutes ago I was doing a little background research on negotiating strategy, and I ran across an article that gave me a laugh. The title was "Why Win-Win Negotiating Is the Surest Way You'll Lose." The writer said that self-made wealthy people are very leery of the win-win strategy and never use it. I'm not sure that I've ever read a more backward or erroneous statement.

The article said that when you play win-win with someone who really wants to win, you end up giving too many concessions in the interest of being nice, you ultimately lose, and it ends up being wimp-win, with you being the wimp.

What? Excuse me, but my half of the win-win strategy says that I *win*. If you give away so much that you lose, then, by definition, you're playing I lose–you win. There are only a couple of situations in which I'll play that game.

The first is when I am willing to take a loss in order that the other person can win simply because of the nature of the relationship. It's rare, but it might come up in a marriage, with a good friend, or with a family member. The thing to be avoided in this situation is that you can't lose and harbor resentment for the loss. If you do that, then it eats away at the relationship and can ultimately cause damage, resulting in a loss for everyone.

The second situation in which I lose–you win can make perfect sense, which I encounter fairly often in business, is when I am happily willing to take a short-term loss in order to get a long-term win. This might be as simple as agreeing to give a client an extra service for a reduced or no fee, which may cost me time and money to do, but which helps improve or solidify the long-term relationship and is ultimately in my own self-interest.

In this scenario, I'm taking that short-term loss for the purpose of creating a long-term and bigger win. So ultimately I'm playing win-win. I use this strategy all the time. I'll gladly "lose" on a short-term transaction in order to win long term. People who fail to see the benefit of this tend to be guilty, as the old saying goes, of "stepping over dollars to pick up nickels."

• **I Win–You Lose.** This is the strategy of the "tough" guy or gal, the bully, or the person who can only think short term. When I teach the win-win strategy in workshops, there are always some people who will say that win-win "sounds good," but it's not the way the real world works. They believe that the real world is one in which, when someone wins, someone has to lose.

Okay, let's think about who we play the game with. Let's start with customers.

Let me get this straight. For me to win, I should make my customer lose? Well, let's all reference our own experiences as customers and see how that strategy invariably plays out.

When you do business with people who make you lose, and especially if they make you lose repeatedly, what do you do? You fire them! You stop doing business with them and you make a point to spread the word about what jerks they are and that no one should ever do business with them.

The real world is much like two little kids playing with a ball. If one of them hogs the ball and won't let the other play, the other quits and goes home. The I win–you lose strategy tends to work only temporarily or short term at best. If you would claim that you have always played to make others lose and that it's worked just fine, I would suggest you would have been infinitely more successful if you had created wins for other people.

If you truly believe that it works in your favor to make the other guy lose, then have at it, and best of luck to you. Sometimes choices come down to "this is how I want to live my life." For me, and for the multitude of successful businesses and individuals that I've worked with over the years, I simply go with the evidence, which is obvious and overwhelming. It's more magnetic to have people want to do business with you than to have people dread doing business with you.

- **I Win–You Win.** This is it. This is the mother lode of all strategies. I honestly believe that this truly is the best idea ever. This is the ultimate magnetic force that attracts business, people, great relationships, money, good fortune, and just about every wonderful thing you can think of. Think I'm overstating things a bit? Not at all. This strategy is, quite simply, the bomb. It trumps all other strategies and consistently beats the I win—you lose strategy in particular.

I Hate to Lose

Don't think for one minute that the people who are masters of the win-win strategy are necessarily overly "nice." If you're nice, that's just a positive byproduct, but it certainly isn't the point. It's about what works. It's about being effective and creating a business that attracts business.

One of the keys to my success is that I hate to lose. I mean I really, really hate to lose. If you ever play a classically competitive sport against me, you'd better bring your "A" game. My long-time friends and family will tell you that I am one of the most competitive people you will ever meet. I play to win, whether it's a game of touch football, billiards, Trivial Pursuit, soccer, checkers, or any other sport or game.

I also hate to lose in the game of business. That's why, more than 35 years after first hearing about the win-win strategy, I am still working to master and refine my use of it. It's the ultimate winning strategy.

I've Developed Reverse Paranoia

In the real world of business, the rules are that for me to get what I want, I must help the other person get what he or she wants. That's just the way business works. The most basic and obvious example of this is with my customers. The only way I stay in business, much less succeed and grow, is to be sure that my customers win. In fact, the rule of success is quite clearly that the ultimate winners and the market leaders are whoever helps the most people win. We all do business with the companies that we feel make us win.

Think of who else you deal with in addition to customers. Employees, coworkers, partners, vendors, the community in general, and on and on. Who on that list do you want to make lose? What possible logic could there be to any strategy other than having them win?

The great thing about leaving a path of winners in your wake is that you build a bank of good will that comes back over and over. I've worked at playing win-win for so many years that I've developed reverse paranoia. I feel like everybody's out to help me.

Of course, in the real world sometimes we have to say no. I've said no to customers in cases where for me to grant their request, I would have had to take too big a loss. But in saying no to them, I tried to create a win for them on some level, even if it was simply to demonstrate they had been heard and understood, and to respectfully explain why I was unable to grant their request. The same goes for employees, partners, vendors, etc.

If there's that rare occasion where the other person is going to take a loss no matter how you handle it, i.e., having to fire an employee, it can still be handled in such a way that you lessen the blow as much as possible through respectful communication. The bottom line and guiding force should always be to avoid a loss and find the win.

"We Make People Lose"

How do you play the game internally in your business? What is your culture when it comes to winners and losers? I worked with a company many years ago that had a clear I win–you lose culture. It was a "survival of the fittest" environment in which everyone was out to undercut everyone else.

I was quite frankly amazed and incredulous that senior leadership there was not only aware of this culture, but encouraged it. The feeling was that it would help create great performance by encouraging the "best" people and ideas to rise to the top. I had one executive say to me, "This is a cutthroat business, and if you can't cut it, then you're out." They may as well have had huge banners hanging on the walls inside and outside the company headquarters that said "We Make People Lose!"

Interestingly, but not surprisingly, the reason that they had called on consultants like me was that the company wasn't performing well, and their competitors were pulling away from them in terms of market share. In reality, it wasn't a "cutthroat" industry at all, but one in which strength of relationships was vitally important to success.

That company, incidentally, ended up going out of business.

This I win–you lose company was drowning in its own self-created pool of bad relationships both inside the company and out. Their failure to understand the true nature of effective competitive strategy in business was their undoing.

It's Like a Cultural Miracle Drug

As magnetic a force as the win-win strategy is for customers, it's just as effective when practiced internally. There's a big difference between companies in which the people continually lift each other up as opposed to cutting each other down. The strategies you employ internally and the way you treat each other is usually a pretty accurate reflection of your external strategy and how you treat customers, vendors, partners, and the community.

The win-win strategy is like a cultural miracle drug that cures a lot of the potential ills that can negatively affect a company's performance. Internal communications, cooperation between departments, creativity, overall employee morale, and more are all positively affected by the use of a win-win strategy internally.

Standing out Like a Sore Thumb

Hopefully you have had the experience of being a part of an organization in which people buy into and embrace a win-win culture. When you've got that kind of mutually supportive environment, everything seems to go more smoothly, and work is more efficient and effective. You've probably also had the experience of that one person or small group of people within the group who insist on playing their "I win–you lose" strategy in contrast to the rest of the team.

I've seen a single person poison the attitudes, morale, and effectiveness of an entire team. I would guess that we all have. I take a pretty hard line about these people. If your stated culture is one of mutual support and cooperation, then the I win–you lose players have to go. It costs too much in terms of coworker morale and inefficiency (i.e. poor communication) to keep them around.

Constructive Disagreements

None of this is to say that there shouldn't be differing opinions or disagreements within a team. On the contrary, a solid win-win culture lets people offer differing points of view openly and honestly in a direct and extremely effective way that ultimately benefits everyone. Win-win means let's get to the best solution. Win-win means I'm willing and even eager to hear your idea, which may be contrary to mine if it can get us to the accomplishment of our goals.

There are dozens of people with whom I've regularly done business for many years and with whom I share a win-win approach. It makes things so easy that it's spoiled me against ever trying to work with anyone who doesn't "get it." I'm amazed by people who are adversarial in their relationships when it makes no sense to be that way.

My good friend and business associate Kris Young and I have worked together for a very long time and have cowritten a book. In our business dealings, we sometimes disagree about what to do or how to do it, and we are very direct and straightforward about these disagreements.

But, because we decided long ago that we are on the same side and that we each want the other to succeed and ultimately win, we can have very constructive disagreements that get us to better decisions and smarter solutions, rather than arguments or personality conflicts. That's one of the main reasons I'm such a fan of the win-win strategy. It helps makes communication, decision making, and, ultimately, performance so much more efficient and effective.

The Ultimate Guideline

What makes the win-win strategy so powerful and effective is its simplicity. I've been using it since I first heard it in 1978 (do the math—that's a long, long time) and it's never failed me. Win-win is the ultimate guideline for attracting business, building a collaborative and effective team, successful negotiating, honest and direct communication, and productive relationships.

In working with tens of thousands of business owners, leaders, managers, and entrepreneurs in my career, win-win is the one idea that I've always said is the best idea I've ever heard. It's not easy to stick with, but it's worth the effort to make it work. The payoff is amazing. It's pure power to those wanting to become magnetic.

- When is it in my best interests, especially long term, to make someone lose?
- (Remember, you don't play the game with your competition. They are a factor, but the game of business is played with customers, coworkers, and partners.)
- What are ways that I can begin to approach everyday situations with a win-win attitude?
- Who are three specific people with whom I will play with a win-win attitude?
- How can we do a better job of making our customers win?
- How can I do a better job of making my coworkers and partners win?

7

Better Beats Different

Don't Strive to Be Different. Be Better. (Now *That's* Different.)

"It's very easy to be different, but very difficult to be better."

—Jony Ive, Chief Design Officer, Apple

Be the Best at What Matters Most—the Only Strategy You'll Ever Need. That's the name of my last book, and it's a bold statement. I wrote the book partly in response to the growing popularity of "wow" factors and "being different" as strategies for success in business. My work with hundreds of businesses tells me that pursuing a strategy of being different almost always turns out to be a wild goose chase that gets you nowhere. It also gets you beaten in the market by competitors who focus on being better.

Let me take the core idea from that book even further and make another bold statement: Better beats different. I would submit to you that this is not my opinion, but the reality of the marketplace.

I'm all for a good "wow" factor, and certainly all for being different, but not at all for the *strategy* of being different. If you want to be a kind of different that counts for something, be better. That's the greatest differentiator in business. The great recession that began in 2008 caused lots of business leaders to look for a way out of their business troubles. Rather than take the path of being better, many of them took the "wow" path, with the hopes that buzzers and bells would create customers and increase business.

Not the Most Unusual Pickup Truck

You can try to compete with your buzzers and bells, but they will be copied by the time you wake up tomorrow. The marketplace makes it incredibly clear: The hardest thing in the world to copy is quality. The most challenging thing to deliver is real value. But that's where the game is won and lost, so that's the place to play. Create value. Be better.

Consumers haven't made the most unusual pickup truck in the world the bestseller, they make the Ford F-Series the best seller for 33 years. It's not a particularly unique truck. Not really different. It's just the one considered the highest quality, best value by the most people. It's a really, really good truck. And that is the differentiating factor. Quality always wins.

The most unusual team doesn't win the Super Bowl, the World Series, or NCAA March Madness. The best team wins. Get a unique uniform—the other team can buy them, too. But have the best players—that can't be copied. What made Michael Jordan different? He was better. That's really, really hard to copy.

Look at Interbrand's list of the top 100 brands in the world. The companies listed there aren't particularly unusual or unique except in that they are . . . well . . . the top 100 brands in the world. They are the best. The also-rans are trying to find an "angle" or a way to be different. Won't help. The only "different" that really counts in the market is value.

Ask Coke or the Toyota Corolla. Different? Not really. Just better. There are lots of soft drinks and certainly lots of compact cars out there. People are drawn to quality and value like metal to, well, a magnet. Being different for the sake of being different will get you short-term business at best. Quality is very, very hard to copy, and it has a long shelf life. Buzzers and bells wear off. Usefulness never does.

The Connection between "Better" and "Distinctive"

Scott McKain is a longtime friend and an expert at helping companies create distinction in every phase of business. He teaches the Ultimate Customer Experience.

I wanted Scott's perspective on the whole idea of being better versus being different. Here's our conversation:

Joe: Scott, what would you say is the connection between being better and being distinctive?

Scott: I would suggest that it would be impossible for an organization—or even an individual professional—to be considered as "distinctive" without being demonstrably better than the competition in at least one area that is of primary importance to customers.

It's an old example, but when Apple introduced the iPod, its success was based upon a fundamental superiority it possessed—it was easier for customers to use than other music players in the marketplace at that time.

Zappos, to use another oft-cited example, is an online retailer—which makes them one of millions. However, they have repeatedly shown how they are demonstrably better at customer service than the competition. So much so, in fact, that Amazon thought it was worth somewhere close to a billion dollars to acquire the company rather than compete with it—and to learn how and why Zappos' customer experience is delivered in a manner superior to Amazon's.

Just being better doesn't ensure that you will become distinctive in the marketplace—but you can't become distinctive without demonstrating to customers that there is something about you that is superior to the other alternatives they have.

Joe: Okay, I'm going to play devil's advocate here and take the side of being different as the way to go. In a marketplace where people see sameness and everything is considered a commodity, what good does it do to be better at the same old thing as everyone else? Isn't being different the best way to stand out? How does just being better get the market's attention?

Scott: First, consider this: Coffee was a commodity, but that didn't stop Starbucks. You can get water out of a fountain for free—but that didn't stop Evian. The tired old excuse that "we are in a commodity business and all our customers want is a cheap price" is only made by tired, old organizations unwilling to make the effort to stand out.

Let's use the water example: How do you make "different" water? Certainly you could manufacture a new soft drink or sports drink—but H_2O is always going to be the formula for water. The only way to stand out and attract customers to pay for something that they can get for free is to be better. Better tasting, more convenient packaging, more healthy because of purity and lack of chemicals, and more accessible would be great starting points.

So how do you get the market's attention? Tell your "better" story.

What is often overlooked is that while different may not always be better, better is always different. If I have a better product because of the reasons stated earlier, I have established that what I'm asking the customer to buy is different—and superior—to other alternatives. If I focus on being better, it's an essential step toward creating distinction. Different will take care of itself.

Finally, better breaks the mold of the same old thing. Enterprise didn't say, "How can we be different from Hertz?" Instead, they asked, "How can we make the car rental experience better for our customers?" They had the idea to bring the car to the customer instead of making the customer go to the rental company's location.

By bringing the car to the customer—"At Enterprise, we pick you up"—they changed the game and became their industry's largest player. Certainly, I'm still doing the same old thing in renting a car. However, by finding a way to do it better and different, Enterprise created distinction for their organization.

Being Better Means Innovation

If you happen to think that having a "better" or value creation strategy isn't dynamic or innovative, think again. It's the one strategy that drives innovation that attracts business. The only reason to innovate is to create value for the customer. Everything else is pointless.

You might have a think lab or "skunkworks" dedicated to free thinking, unfettered imagination, and over-the-edge experimentation. Good for you. I'm for it. And the ultimate purpose of all of that free thinking is to lead to improvements and innovations that benefit a customer.

The best at anything are in constant forward motion, always moving forward toward "make it even better," always innovating in the interest of creating value for the customer. In fact, it's impossible to sustain a quality or value advantage without that constant innovation. The bar of customer expectations will always be raised, and at least some of your competition will always be trying to match and beat your value.

To stay in front, all you have to do is work harder, be smarter, and be better.

It's the path less taken because it's the most challenging route to success. But the clichés are true. There is no short cut to success.

- What are the basics of our business? How can we become better at each of them?
- How can we, like Apple products are easier to use, become easier to do business with?
- How can we, like Zappos, become better at customer service?
- Evian and Starbucks refused to believe that "lowest price" was the determining factor in their commodity-based businesses. What are we doing to differentiate ourselves out of the commodity/lowest price trap?
- What makes us better than our competition? Are we, in fact, better than our competition? How? How can we prove that we are? What are we willing and/or able to do that our competition is not willing and/or able to do?

8

From Magnetic to Irrelevant

The Greatest Threat

In a world that doesn't just change quickly, but continuously, the greatest threat to your marketplace viability may very well be irrelevance. The graveyard of failed businesses is filled with companies that went from magnetic to irrelevant. It can be a gradual slide into irrelevance in which the company sees customers and revenue slipping away little by little, or it can be a sudden realization one day that it's just over—you simply stopped mattering.

Witness Radio Shack's long, slow, painful slide from magnetic to irrelevant.

It was kind of like the old story of putting a frog in a pan of water that slowly, degree by degree, became hot enough to kill him. The frog never jumped out because it was so gradual. Don't be the frog. Take action with your business long before the water's too hot!

Wild for CB Radios

It's likely that very few people reading this are old enough to remember CB radios, but trust me, it was a wildly popular fad in the late 1960s. Radio Shack not only jumped on that train but was the locomotive for it. Tens of thousands of people flocked to Radio Shack stores to get their CB radio, and the company was not only relevant, but vitally relevant to this huge consumer trend.

When CB radios began to lose popularity, Radio Shack was ahead of the curve and totally relevant in the next great consumer electronics craze, the personal computer. Again, not many remember the days of the TRS-80, the first mass-produced personal computer. Radio Shack made it and made millions from selling it.

The computer hardware business became unprofitable, Radio Shack got out of it, and they were right there for the next big thing—cell phones. In fact, Radio Shack became the go-to place for cell phones. But the mobile carriers moved away from using Radio Shack and opened their own stores. And that was the end of that.

The rise of the cell phone also made a lot of the products sold by Radio Shack irrelevant. GPS devices, voice recorders, camcorders, and answering machines were all replaced by that one cell phone in your pocket. From an inventory standpoint, Radio Shack was becoming a confused mess with no identity.

Next up in consumer electronics was e-commerce. You could now buy products online from Target, Walmart, Best Buy, and many others right from their websites. The Radio Shack website gave consumers a store locator. Radio Shack did finally begin to offer a ship-to-store program, in which consumers could order products online and pick them up at the nearest store. But with Amazon and everyone else shipping straight to the consumer's home and doing it with great speed, The Shack (as the company had lamely begun to call itself) was simply irrelevant.

Radio Shack was unable to take advantage of what was seemingly its best shot at relevance, which was serving the emerging "maker" community. These are electronics enthusiasts who make their own devices. It could have been an opportunity, but somehow it just slipped away.

Next stop for Radio Shack: bankruptcy.

Dogs are Loyal. Customers Aren't.

There was a great TV commercial with two young guys on an elevator, each of them totally focused on their smartphones, obviously engrossed by their choice of social media. One of them, without looking up, asks the other, "Hey man, you on Woo Woo?" The other responds, without looking up, "Yeah, man. Everybody's on Woo Woo." Later the two are on the elevator again. One asks, "You still on Woo Woo?" The other says, "No, man. My mom's on Woo Woo."

The days of customers staying loyal to companies for long periods of time are numbered. The amount of trust consumers put in brands is steadily decreasing, and a typical consumer will now switch brands without hesitation if they get a better offer or if that brand becomes irrelevant to the consumer.

There's only one way to defy the declining loyalty of customers. You have to start over every day and re-earn it. One mistake that many businesses are making is to see the defection of their customers as a marketing challenge. Usually it's not. It's a value challenge. Customers leave because they don't see the value anymore.

There are any number of reasons that you might lose customers or see a slowdown in your ability to attract new customers. In addition to irrelevance, some of them are:

- They didn't know. Now they do.

   Your product, service, and price is being instantly compared to your competitor's. Anyone with a smartphone, and that's everyone, can check the marketplace to compare anything with everything. Car buyers now often know more about the cars they buy than the car salespeople do.
- Your competition is everyone.

   You may think that because you provide the best service in your industry, it makes you bulletproof against customer defections. Think again. Your service and everything you do is compared to best-in-class companies across the spectrum.

If my customers get more personal treatment from their dry cleaners, they are going to wonder why I'm not willing to give them the same thing.
- You are disconnected internally.

See the chapter You're Fired! for my phone company example. I was bounced from department to department, and the lack of information that these employees had about my situation was staggering. One department didn't know what the other had said or was doing. A lack of communication, working in "silos," or a failure of your people to understand one another's jobs can result in your customers thinking that you are either incompetent or, worse, that you don't care.

Think Again

If you are thinking to yourself, "These stories about companies like Radio Shack are interesting, but they don't have anything to do with me," think again. I would say that as a business writer, consultant, and speaker, I'm about as different a business entity from Radio Shack, Subway, and as anyone or anything could be.

But I do have one thing in common with Radio Shack, you, and every other business: the fundamental need to stay relevant. For all of us, relevance is the most important survival factor in business. The moment you begin to matter less to your customers, that's the moment that you begin going out of business.

Keep your magnet for attracting business strong by staying vitally relevant to your customers.

- If we do not change, what will make us irrelevant to our customers? Why will we stop mattering to them?
- What is working for us now that is likely to stop working in the future?
- Which of our competitors is doing the best job of changing to meet customers' future wants and needs?
- Which of our competitors are we most often compared to? How might we be at risk of losing in that comparison?
- If we claim to be "world class," how do we compare to the best businesses in the world?
- Do all parts of our business, and all of the people in it, work together as one? Do we all know and understand one another's jobs and functions? Do we ever work against each other, even without intending to?

9
Never Stop Improving

"The moment you think you know everything, you're already done as a chef. You should just quit."

—Niki Nakayama, owner/chef, n/naka restaurant, Los Angeles

You Could Just Do This, and You'd Succeed

Many successful businesspeople (and I agree with them) believe that if you're good at what you do and there's a market for what you do, you could just do this and you'd be successful: Never stop improving.

My guess is that almost all of the people who claim that they are always improving really aren't. They may be thinking about it, and I'll bet they're talking about it, but they're probably not really doing it.

When people tell me that they believe in continuous improvement, I ask them what they did last Thursday that made them better than they were last Wednesday. It's exceptionally rare that anyone is ever anything but completely stumped by that question. They remember that last Thursday was really busy and everyone was slammed and doing all they could just to keep up with what was going on. No one really had time to actually get better at anything. And the problem is that that's going to probably be true for every day. They were too busy to get better.

Lip Service

Nothing gets more lip service than the idea of continuous improvement. Everyone is for it. It's unanimous. Everyone agrees with the idea that constant and continuous improvement is essential to staying competitive.

And hardly anyone does it.

Most people try to improve occasionally, as a project, but rarely do we make the idea of always getting better a permanent and ever-present part of our thinking. The idea of constant improvement should always be in our thinking, strategies, and actions, not as a distraction from what we're doing, but as a natural part of our consciousness about it.

When we become intentional about creating an awareness of always getting better as a part of the way we do everything, then it becomes much easier to identify the "what" and "how" to get better. We usually set aside time to think about getting better, and in a vacuum, it's hard to do. Better to think about it every day, as a natural part of what we do, as natural as turning on the lights in the morning. Over the years I have noticed that top performers not only subscribe to the idea of continuous improvement, but have learned how to build identification of what to improve and how to improve into their work.

A Daily Ritual

Perhaps the simplest process for always getting better is to take a few minutes at the end of each day to synthesize and collect your thoughts from the day about how things could have gone better. I've had people ranging from airline pilots and stockbrokers to managers in manufacturing and ministers tell me that part of their daily work ritual is to take 15 minutes at the end of each day for reflection on what could have gone better.

It starts with a willingness to question everything. You have to look critically at current practices and "the way we do things here" with an eye toward improvement if you are going to move forward. The great danger lies in the assumption that things are fine just the way they are. No matter how good something is, be it a process, a product, a practice, a standard, an attitude, or absolutely anything else—it can always be better.

Many people are familiar with the Japanese concept of *kaizen*, meaning small improvements and changes on a regular basis. A concept I heard years ago in association with Toyota was "permanent dissatisfaction." While that might have a negative connotation at first, it really is at the core of having a positive attitude about change and always getting better. Never be satisfied or complacent about the way things are. Always look to improve the quality of every aspect of what you do.

Jazz musician Wynton Marsalis put it this way: "If you don't feel any tension in what you're doing, then you're not serious about it. You have to be able to create new things to be successful, and the new things come from constantly questioning what you're already doing."

Without a Process It's Just a Slogan

It's easy to fall into the trap of confusing *talking* about always getting better with the actual reality of *doing* the things that will actually create improvements. I have seen countless meetings in which continuous improvement was talked about as if it were at the core of the organization's values. After the meeting everyone went back to work and did things the way they had always done them.

Without a process for change, it's just a slogan.

You Have to Get Specific

I took my daughter to the doctor to see about some minor but persistent ailment she was experiencing. At the check-in window there was a poster that I couldn't help but notice.

"We are dedicated to continuous improvement. We are dedicated to 100 percent of our patients having an excellent experience 100 percent of the time. 97 percent of our patients say they would recommend us and we want that to continue (and improve).

Right now we are working on:

- Expanding your ability to contact us after hours.
- Informing you when your appointment is delayed.
- Improving billing and insurance assistance.
- Simplifying the process of referring you to a specialist.

Let us know how we're doing either in person or on our website. We need your feedback and input if we're going to get better. More improvements are on the way."

Of course, if printing up the sign were as far as things had gotten, then they would have been stuck in slogan mode. I asked the woman at the front desk about the initiatives on the sign, and she immediately began to tell me, with enthusiasm, about some of the steps they were taking to make the improvements real. She further told me that they had committed to having everyone on the staff always be on the lookout for anything they did that could be improved. These areas for improvement were then taken to the next step, which is process and action. Without a process for change, continuous improvement is just a slogan.

That's the way it's done. You don't have a staff meeting and say "let's always get better at everything we do" then adjourn the meeting and go back to what you've always done. You get specific about what improvements and changes to make; you assign responsibility, accountability, and the authority to take necessary actions; you allocate a budget if necessary; you create a schedule for completion; and you move forward until it's done.

Then you acknowledge that you're never really done, because what you just improved can be made better, and there's always other things to improve, as well.

You have to be going through a neverending cycle of:

- Now: our present condition
- Next: the desired state
- New: how to reach that state

The critical part is "how to reach that state." Taking action is the only thing that gives value to your ideas about improvement.

If It's Worth Doing, It's Worth Doing Wrong

G. K. Chesterton, in his book *What's Wrong with the World*, said: "If it's worth doing, it's worth doing badly." My friend Arnie Malham changed it to wording that I like better when he said, "If it's worth doing, it's worth doing wrong."

What in the world does that mean? It means that you should take action even if you know you're not going to do it perfectly. It means that you move forward even if you know you'll only get to 50 percent of the solution. It means that doing something in the interest of getting better beats doing nothing, because we live in a world where doing nothing means certain defeat.

All Sorts of Things Occur

W. H. Murray was a Scottish mountaineer and writer. Near the beginning of his 1951 book *The Scottish Himalayan Expedition* is a passage that captures the power of taking action:

> . . . (B)ut when I said that nothing had been done I erred in one important matter. We had definitely committed ourselves and were

halfway out of our ruts. We had put down our passage money—booked a sailing to Bombay. This may sound too simple, but is great in consequence. Until one is committed, there is hesitancy, the chance to draw back, always ineffectiveness. Concerning all acts of initiative (and creation), there is one elementary truth, the ignorance of which kills countless ideas and splendid plans: that the moment one definitely commits oneself, then Providence moves too. All sorts of things occur to help one that would never otherwise have occurred. A whole stream of events issues from the decision, raising in one's favor all manner of unforeseen incidents and meetings and material assistance, which no man could have dreamt would have come his way. I learned a deep respect for one of Goethe's couplets:

Whatever you can do or dream you can, begin it.

Boldness has genius, power and magic in it!

It Can Always Be Better

Years ago I gave a speech at the National Speakers Association's annual convention. It was a keynote speech in front of about 2,000 of my professional colleagues and friends, almost all of whom are in the same business as me. For the most part, they are all very good at what they do, and some of them are intimidatingly good. This was my audience.

I had prepared for this speech for well over a year and had put more effort and intention into it than any speech I'd ever delivered in my life. We've all experienced the feeling of being at the right place at the right time, and that's what happened to me that morning. The speech worked beyond what I had expected or even hoped for, and I was ecstatic.

My mind is wired for constant improvement. I know it is because I wired it that way. It was the most natural thing in the world for me to review that very successful speech and look for ways that it could have been better. I identified five very specific moments in the speech that I felt could have gone better and been more effective, and I further identified how I would change it to make those improvements real.

This was a one-time-only speech for that one audience, but I still went through the process of how to improve it, because that process empowers me. That process of continuous improvement, or my own version of Toyota's state of "permanent dissatisfaction," is one of my greatest competitive strengths.

"Always improving my product" is one of the three most important things I do every single day (see the chapter "The Three Things You Must Get Right"). A dedication to continuous improvement is the single most important factor in keeping my business successful for over 30 years in the face of constant, intense, and every talented competition.

Always get better. Be relentless, consistent, and constant about it.

- Do we believe that, in order to be competitive, we have to be better tomorrow than we were today?
- If so, what specific improvement did we make yesterday over where we were the day before?
- Are we willing to make constant improvement a process and part of what we do all day long, every single day, rather than a project that we try and do occasionally?
- Have we gotten too comfortable with what has worked for us up to this point?
- What do we do extremely well that we can improve?
- What do we do now that we are willing to let go of?

(continued)

(*continued*)

- If we have identified something we want to improve, have we taken the steps necessary to make that more than an idea? Are we taking action? Has someone been given the responsibility and authority to make it happen? Do we have a plan and a schedule in place to achieve the improvement? Do we have a way to measure the improvement?
- What is something that I, personally, will commit to improving on immediately?

10

The Magnetic Mind-Set

Common Threads

Successful leaders and top performers in business tend to think alike. They may be completely different in style, personality, strategies, and tactics, but there are common threads in the mind-sets of people who consistently do well in business.

Strategies and tactics will ultimately fail unless they are built on a mind-set, a way of thinking about your business that provides both stability and flexibility. Part of that mind-set is going to be about values, and your culture will ultimately come from there. But it's important to develop an attitude that creates magnetism and the ability to attract business. That's mind-set.

Here are three key characteristics of the magnetic mind-set:

1. I Believe That my Competition is Really Good at What They do, and That They are Always Gaining on me, are Even with me, or Have Passed me

A classic rookie mistake is to underestimate your competition and, sadly, it is one of the most common weaknesses I see in businesses of all kinds. I refer to it as a rookie mistake because it's the kind of thing that someone who doesn't know any better would do, but the sad fact is that I see experienced business-people do it all the time.

A leading independent grocery store had a nationally known competitor moving into their market. There were some in the organization who were like little kids who had closed their eyes, put their hands over their ears, and were yelling "I can't hear you! I can't hear you!" over and over. They didn't want to acknowledge reality, which was that, even as successful as they had always been, this was a serious competitive threat, and they'd better up their game or suffer the consequences.

If your competition truly is inept, ineffective, and no good, then you can coast. You obviously have all the customers and there's no need for you to ever be any better than you are now, and certainly no need to change. There's also no need for you to ever take hallucinogenic drugs because you are living in a seriously altered space that bears no resemblance to the real world.

The self-delusional belief that you're the only one who is good at what you do is a serious competitive weakness, and it can kill your business. Ineffective, mediocre business practitioners limit their view of reality with blinders that block the truth, which is that yes, you do have competition, and yes, they are good at what they do. Truly effective business leaders have 20/20 vision about their competitors, and they use that awareness to their advantage.

I recently had the opportunity to spend time with some of Starbucks' top leaders. If ever there was a company that has dominated its market, Starbucks is it. Yet the thing I heard that has stuck with me since that meeting was a statement made by one of those leaders, who said, "The one thing we've never been is complacent. You're only as good as the next thing you do. We fear every and any competitor."

Let me tell you about the world I live in. My competitors are not just good; they are very, very good. I sometimes just shake my head at the quality and excellence of their work. For me to even be competitive with them, much less win, I have to constantly get better at what I do. Every great company I have ever worked with has been very clear about acknowledging their competitors' strengths. It's very bad business to ever underestimate your competition, and those who do so generally tend to be at the back of the pack. Market leaders use the strength of competitors as motivators for innovation, improvement, positive change, and growth.

It's good to know your own strengths, and I love celebrating victories. But in addition to counting the reasons that you think you will win, you'd better devote at least as much time, thought, and energy to considering all the ways you could possibly lose. Regularly go through the exercise of "what could cause us to stop winning new customers or even cause us to lose existing customers?" Think about "what could cause our existing customers to lose their enthusiasm for recommending us?"

Identify the competitive threats, then take action to neutralize them. Never, ever get caught in the trap of believing that your competition is no good. And if they really aren't, pretend that they are. Somewhere out there is someone or something looking to take your business down. Conduct your business accordingly. I know I do.

I run in a positive state of "scared" all the time. I believe that if I don't do something significant to improve and get better, and do it now, I'll soon be out of business. I agree with John Burke, president of high-performance bicycle manufacturing company Trek, when he said, "The secret is always running the business like you're two touchdowns behind. We'll always do better if we have a little bit of fear and a sense of urgency."

2. I Don't Apologize to Customers, Because I Don't do Things That I Have to Apologize for

Your immediate reaction and objection to this may understandably be: "But there's no way to get everything right 100 percent of the time. Mistakes will be made. You just have to accept that." I'm with you right up until the point where you say "you just have to accept that."

As a customer, I hate it when a manager feels that she has to apologize to me, because that means that something has gone wrong and it was usually something completely avoidable. There are managers who spend way too much time apologizing when they should be spending that time training their people or fixing their processes so that they won't have to be apologizing.

I will readily admit that my "I don't apologize to customers, because I don't do things that I have to apologize for" is very much an aspirational statement. Yes, things go wrong. Yes, mistakes are made. But I hate having to apologize to my clients *so* much that I wage a neverending war on mistakes and the faulty processes that can produce them.

It's a powerful thing to have a "no stupid mistakes—no defects—no surprises" policy that becomes part of the DNA of your team. There's the old saying, "Amateurs work until they get it right. Professionals work until they can't get it wrong." That's what you aspire to. You work every day to get to the point that your team doesn't know how to get it wrong.

Here's a good place to start. Look for any pattern of mistakes or things for which you find yourself apologizing to customers on a regular basis. If there's something that happens like clockwork at least once a month, then you've almost certainly got either a process problem or a training problem.

If and when you do find yourself in a situation where something went wrong and you feel the need to apologize to a customer, the apology shouldn't be your top priority. Do the apology sincerely and quickly. Remember that you can't fake sincerity. If you don't mean it from your heart, the customer will know it and you're dead. People resent fake apologies, and they can spot them a mile away.

But if you are, in fact, sincere with your apology, then move quickly to the next step, which should be your top priority. You will now make up for whatever went wrong with a solution and a demonstration of good will that overwhelms the customer to the point that they are amazed. They will leave the situation as your greatest advocate, and the positive word of mouth will be extraordinary.

I once gave a speech for which the client had ordered 600 copies of one of my books to distribute to the attendees at the event. We shipped the wrong book. The client was upset. Trust me when I say that's an understatement. I apologized and then immediately made this offer: Their attendees can keep the 600 mistakenly shipped books at no charge. We will ship a copy of the book that was supposed to have been shipped to each attendee individually. There will be no charge for those books or for the shipping.

What I was offering was many thousands of dollars worth of solution and a tsunami of corrective action in a way that stunned the client. She asked to think about it and let me know the next morning, when I would be giving the speech. That next day she said that just giving everyone the book that had been shipped at no charge was plenty.

Two other factors in this misadventure are worth mentioning. The speech I gave was a huge hit with her attendees. It was vitally important in this case (as it is in every case) for me to do a great job on the core product, which was the speech. The other factor is that this speech had been booked through a bureau partner that I work with often. My solution for the client was also done with my relationship with that bureau in mind.

Afterward my contact at the bureau said, "We were never worried about it. We knew you'd handle it perfectly." That's magnetic.

My solution cost me a whopping lot of money, but it preserved two important relationships and, as I am a devoted adherent to the win-win philosophy of business, it was the only way for me to handle it. I lost short term in a transactional "dollars" sense. But I won big time long term on the relationship level. Lesson: Don't step over dollars to pick up nickels. I'll take a short-term loss for a long-term gain every single time.

Let me be clear about something. I'm not bragging. This isn't about me being a swell guy. This is about what works in business. There are countless others in business who do all of this better than I do. I aspire to learn from them. I was not making a sacrifice by giving the client those 600 books for free. I was making a bottom line, future revenue, future growth business decision that was logical and necessary for me to get what I wanted.

This book isn't about feeling good by being nice. This book is about feeling good by making a profit and growing a business.

3. I Say "No" to a Lot of Potential Customers and Business

Any revenue is better than no revenue, right? No, not right. Not right at all. Sometimes there are sources of revenue that will kill your business. Learning when to say no is one of the most essential mind-sets to creating a magnetic business.

My favorite Warren Buffett quote is, "The difference between successful people and very successful people is that very successful people say 'no' to almost everything." It took me a long time to learn the positive business growth power of saying no, and it's something I wish I had learned much sooner than I did. Today I say no to a lot of the potential customers that come my way, because they don't make it through the filter that helps us find the right fit.

It often comes down to this—just because you *could* do business with a customer doesn't mean that you *should* do business with that customer. When your business is brand new, it's hard to turn business away, and I openly admit that I took jobs that were more than a stretch for me. They were jobs that I shouldn't have taken on. But that's part of the learning curve. The key is to be sure that you do learn that lesson and begin to build your filter to make sure that you only do business with customers who are the right fit.

For my business, there are two main parts to my filter that will cause me to say no to potential customers who are ready and willing to give me their money. There is what I call the business filter, and then there's the personal filter. Just one "bad mark" in either of those filters can be enough for me to say no.

Everyone will have to set their own parameters for what's a good or bad match in terms of their business, but it's often a matter of being able to distinguish between what you "could" do and what you "should" do. Using my business as an example, I recently got a call asking if I'd work with a corporate group who needed expertise in execution strategies. I could have put a program together for them, but it would have taken me out of the real strengths and expertise that I have. I referred the group to my friend Randy Pennington, who has expertise in that area which far surpasses mine, making him a much better match.

I accomplished two things with that referral. I avoided the stress and distraction that would have come from trying to fit a square peg into a round hole. I also gained credibility and good feelings from the client, who will be happy with Randy and will thus be happy with me. My hope and expectation is that now I am on their list for future consideration if it's a proper fit.

My friend Jane Atkinson is a respected career and strategy coach to professional speakers. Jane's business filter caused her to make a significant policy change in her business recently. Here's what Jane said about her decision:

"For several years I was offering my coaching clients payment plans that would bill their credit card monthly over the course of a year. I thought it might be good for cash flow and they would appreciate the option to spread the payments out. However, time went by and I realized my team and I were spending far too much time chasing after credit card issues. With all of the fraud in Canada and the U.S., cards were being cancelled all of the time. Sometimes the same client would change cards three times in a year. And with cards expiring, we were running around in circles. I didn't want to be in the credit card business, I wanted to be a coach. So I decided to remove all of the long-term options off of the website."

The obvious consideration for Jane had to be that she might lose some clients who would only hire her if they could make payments spread out over time. I asked Jane about it:

"I haven't heard anyone complain about it yet, and no has asked for extra time in paying so far, although it's just been a few months. But when a client is perfect for me, part of the criteria is that they can easily afford my services."

Jane nails it when she talks about "part of the criteria." That's the filter. Almost every kind of business has to have a filter, or set criteria, for customers, or it will find itself wasting time, effort, energy, and emotion trying to make the wrong customers "fit." It's a losing battle.

There's a simple, powerful lesson and guideline here for all businesses. Don't say yes to customers who will take much more time or attention than the revenue they produce will justify. We can all point to our own list of time-consuming and stress-producing customers from our past. Please learn the lessons that those mistakes taught you and don't make that mistake again.

Speaking of stress, let's look at the personal filter as a way to weed out customers who would be a bad fit. Over the years, my own personal filter has gotten tighter in terms of who gets through. Luckily for me, the vast majority of people and companies who approach me to do business turn out to be delightful and a pleasure to work with. Maybe I've gotten somewhat spoiled by that, but I am now squarely in the space where I will not work with anyone who falls into my "life's too short" category.

You know what I'm talking about. It's that customer who causes so much stress that whatever amount of money they're giving you simply isn't worth the wear and tear that they put you through. From both a quality of life and also from a smart business perspective, I advise you to set the parameters on your personal filter clearly and strictly, and to never work with jerks again. Just say no.

I did a keynote presentation for a group years ago that proved to be the ultimate example of a "red flag" client. The night before the presentation I met with my main client contact to do a final check-in, and that's when he started in with his list of changes, objections, doubts, fears, and borderline insults. In the interest of doing the best job possible for the organization, I stuck to my guns on what I thought would be most effective.

The next morning I did the presentation to what was a wonderful group of business executives, and afterward my bad-natured contact showered me with praise. Two weeks later, we received an invitation for me to speak at two overseas events for the group, at my full fee for out-of-the-country work, which isn't cheap.

I didn't have to think twice about my answer: "No, thank you." My strong sense of this individual was that he would pull the same power-trip stunts again at any future event, and he clearly fell into the "life's too short" category for me to every do business with.

I can always find more clients, and ones who are a pleasure to work with, not a misery. My experience has been that when you say no to the wrong people, it opens up the space for the right people to come in.

Years ago I was impressed by the guiding statement of business adopted by a new advertising firm. Their four rules of doing business were:

1. Do great work.
2. Make money.
3. Have fun.
4. Don't work with people you can't stand.

It takes courage to abide by that fourth rule, but in the long run, it's worth it.

- Do we ever underestimate our competition?
- Which of our competitors do we need to have a healthy fear of?
- Where might the next competitive threat to our business come from?
- Where do we make too many mistakes with customers?
- Do we solve customer complaints in a way that wins that customer forever?
- Are we solving problems too often when we should be improving faulty processes, training, etc., that are causing the problems in the first place?
- Do we have customers we shouldn't be doing business with?
- Do we have a filter in place that keeps us from doing business with the wrong customers?

11

The St. Paul Saints

It's All Word of Mouth

Not Your Usual Case Study

I wanted to find a business that absolutely captured the idea of being magnetic. It needed to be an organization that was great at attracting business. It had to be a case study that we could all learn from. What I found is not your usual case study: I found the St. Paul Saints. In them, I also found some fundamental and effective ideas for any business that wants to become magnetic.

There's a great learning advantage in using examples far removed from our usual business experience. Looking at a baseball organization takes me out of the assumptions that I have about how my own business and those similar to it are supposed to work. I look at the magnetic qualities of the St. Paul Saints and the positive bottom line results that they create, then work backward, asking, "How do they do it?" From there, it's adaptive innovation to apply the same principles to my own business.

Fiercely Loyal Customers Year in and Year Out

Mike Veeck is the driving force behind the St. Paul Saints. Those of you who are fans of professional baseball will recognize the name, if not because of Mike's career, then certainly because of his father, the legendary Bill Veeck.

The leadership and employees of the St. Paul Saints are masters of the win-win strategy (see the chapter The Best Idea Ever). Their customers have almost unlimited choices about how and where to spend their time and money. They could go to the baseball game, or they could go to:

- the movies
- a concert
- the mall

- a restaurant
- the lake
- a friend's house
- the library
- the bowling alley
- the computer screen
- a book
- a bar
- or just stay home

I could go on and on with an unlimited list of choices that St. Paul Saints customers have. But what they choose to do, often enough to make this business a goldmine, is go to the baseball game. More of them than you might think aren't even true baseball fans. But they love going to the ballpark and soaking up the experience that is a St. Paul Saints baseball game.

The reason they go to St. Paul Saints games is that Veeck and company make sure that, regardless of which team wins the game, their customers always win. They get greater value, more bang for their buck, more customer satisfaction, and have more fun at the game than they can have anywhere else.

The St. Paul Saints totally understand that equation.

The Most Spectacular Experience You Can Have

One of the owners of the St. Paul Saints is Bill Murray. Yes, *that* Bill Murray. On the St. Paul Saints website, he is officially listed as "Team Psychologist." In an interview with *Minnesota Business Magazine*, Murray talked about how he connected with Mike Veeck: "We traveled parallel lines. My connection with the Cubs is from birth, his goes back to his grandfather who was the president of the Cubs. Michael was in Florida and we started up with a little Florida team. The Saints have been our greatest achievement. It's the most spectacular experience you can have as a baseball fan."

The idea here is to wrap the work that you do for your customers with an experience that puts you, to quote the title of one of my previous books, in a "category of one." Of course, you have to begin with being the best at whatever your core value proposition is, but if you can then expand the experience to something unexpected, that's when you can get to your version of spectacular.

"A Whole New Ballgame"

"A Whole New Ballgame"—That was the banner headline for the story that took up most of the front page of the *St. Paul Pioneer Press* newspaper. Not the sports page, mind you, but the front page. It was the morning after the opening season game for the St. Paul Saints, which I had flown to St. Paul, Minnesota from Nashville to see because I wanted to know, firsthand, what all the fuss was about.

I'm not a big-time baseball fan, but I am a big-time business fan, and for years I had heard about this minor league baseball team in St. Paul that had an amazing reputation for building and, much more important, keeping and growing an intensely enthusiastic and loyal fan base. I wanted to find out about the culture and strategies that had made this organization so successful for so long.

I came away with four rock-solid ideas.

1. Break Down the Limits. (Bad Karaoke, Great Beer, Bill Murray, and Massages From a Nun.)

The *St. Paul Pioneer Press* said this about the St. Paul Saints experience: "It's like going to a ballgame but not being limited to going to a ballgame." That's it. That's what I want for my business. I want to break down limits. But what did that mean for the St. Paul Saints?

So there's a baseball game going on, and the team is fun to watch. They're a good team, and the game is, of course, the core of what's being offered by the St. Paul Saints. Beyond the game, though, is this incredible experience that acts as a megamagnet for the legions of Saints fans. It is, as the newspaper said, not limited to a ballgame.

I encourage you to check out the website saintsbaseball.com to get at least a taste of what the experience is all about. From my perspective as a customer, here are just a few of the things that caught my attention at the season-opening game and made me think about the experience that I create for my own customers:

- a brand spanking new, knock-your-socks-off, state-of-the-art stadium;
- the incredible food and craft beer choices from the friendliest, most customer-focused vendors that you can imagine;
- haircuts available from "Mr. B";
- Sister Rosalind Gefre, the nun who wanders the stands offering shoulder massages;
- the Bill Murray sightings (he attends the games when he can and has been known to act as a ticket-taker for the fans as they enter the ballpark);
- the PA announcers who are as funny as any comedy team anywhere;
- the pig—this year it's Pablo Pigasso—who delivers the game baseballs to the umpires before the start of the game;
- and my favorite, the Bad Karaoke singing between innings from "A Real Japanese Guy" (the night I was there he led the stadium in singing "Feels Like The First Time" by Foreigner). He was off-key and truly a pretty bad singer and more fun than you can imagine.

So what does any of this have to do with your business or mine? Simply this: Do you want your customers to love doing business with you? Of course you do. So do I. The customers of the St. Paul Saints love them. They love them because they get much more than you'd ever expect from a baseball game. The normal limits and expectations have been exceeded.

Do your clients or customers get much more than anyone would ever expect from a business like yours?

I want to have my own version of the Bad Karaoke guy in the sense that I want to offer something beyond my core product that my customers will love, remember, and want more of. I want to be on my customers' "favorites" lists. And most of all, I want my customers to talk about me and create a positive word-of-mouth buzz like the Saints' customers create about them.

2. Hire Great People and Get Out of Their Way

At the game, I got to spend some time with Mike Veeck. I asked him about what made this whole magnificent organization work. He talked about the people in the organization and what they try to accomplish for the fans. He summed it up with, "Hire great people and get out of their way."

If I had gotten nothing else from Mike, that simple idea was enough to justify the trip. Of course it's basic, but like most basic, great ideas, few people have the wisdom to follow it. Mike understands that if you lay the foundation of a great culture, built on the right values, then you can turn it over to the people in the organization and they'll do the right things.

In my ballpark conversation with Mike, he gave all the credit for the success of the Saints to his employees. I recommend that you read Mike's book *Fun Is Good*, in which he makes it clear that it's all about the players on the team. Not just the players on the baseball team, but the players throughout the organization who organize, manage, maintain, and most important, entertain for the benefit of their customers.

As I talked with Mike, his co-owner Bill Murray sat a few seats away obviously enjoying the game and everything around him. Murray takes great delight and pride in the St. Paul Saints, and his appreciation for their employees is obvious. In his interview with *Minnesota Business Magazine*, Murray gave an example of how the employees make the Saints the success that they are. "There's one person who works for us, Annie Huidekoper, and she's the most passionate, enthusiastic person we have," Murray said. "She's committed to the fans' experience and that legitimizes the whole enterprise."

3. Fun is Good

"Fun is good." This is the philosophy of the St. Paul Saints, and it's what drives just about everything that Mike Veeck does in his business and his life. In his book *Fun Is Good* Mike wrote about that philosophy:

> *You don't have to own a baseball team to benefit from* Fun Is Good. *In fact, anyone who gauges the business success of our baseball teams by our promotions is missing the point. After all, everyone in minor league baseball relies on cheap theatrics because we have no big-name ballplayers to promote.*
>
> *What makes us successful—and what I would argue makes any company successful—is not necessarily a superior product. (Heck, we have an inherently inferior product: minor league and independent league baseball.) But we succeed on a level where our bigger, well-heeled brethren in the major leagues do not. We do so by providing superior customer service and creating fun in the workplace.*

It's a simple formula, but one applied not nearly enough in American business.

The "fun is good" formula is indeed one that can be applied to any business. Mike and his team are taking it to businesses of all kinds through their "Fun Is Good" presentations and workshop sessions. The idea is that "When Fun Is Good, Performance Gets Better! A Different Way To Bring Fun, Employee Engagement and Profitability Into The Workplace." Check it out at funisgoodteam.com.

4. It's All Word of Mouth

The final wrap-up idea that Mike Veeck had for me about the key to success was this: "It's all word of mouth."

The St. Paul Saints are one of those businesses that have figured it out. If the work you do is good enough, the work itself becomes your marketing. Your customers' satisfaction becomes the fuel that drives the most powerful business marketing power ever known: word of mouth.

Here's your challenge and opportunity—to follow the example of Mike Veeck and the St. Paul Saints in finding your version of going beyond the traditional expectations of people or businesses who do what you do. Redefine it. Expand the idea of what you can be and mean to your customers.

Creating, as Bill Murray said, a "most spectacular experience" for your customers doesn't mean you have to be loud or showy about it. It's not about hyperbole. Quite the opposite. Your version of the St. Paul Saints kind of magnetism may be quiet and calm, and just as effective at creating something spectacular for your customers.

- Where do you get your new ideas?
- Do you regularly bring new ideas to your business from organizations that are unlike yours?
- If not, I repeat, where do you get your new ideas?
- Do you make the experience of doing business with you greater than what your customers expected? If so, how? If not, how could you begin?
- How do you expand the limits of how people normally think of a business like yours?
- Do you hire great people and then get out of their way?
- Is your business fun? Do your customers have fun doing business with you? Do your employees have fun at work?
- If you think having "fun" isn't appropriate for your business, fine. Do you want your customers to love doing business with you? How do you make sure that happens?
- Do you want your employees to love their jobs? How do you make sure that happens?
- Is the experience of doing business with you your best marketing? If not, why not?

12

A Magnet Needs a Market

It Seemed Like Such a Good Idea at the Time

Whether you're considering starting a new business or expanding your existing business, there are obvious but often overlooked factors that will be key in determining your success or failure. Rarely, if ever, is any business idea a sure thing, and I've got plenty of personal experience in launching ideas that sank like rocks thrown into a pond.

Picture this: You've come up with an idea for the best magnet ever. Everyone tells you that your magnet will be able to pull metal of all kinds from long distances. Your magnet will be absolutely covered up.

You finish your magnet, put it on a table with metal balls and shavings all around, and . . . nothing. They are so close that they are almost touching your magnet but nothing is making the slightest move toward it.

In spite of all the planing and enthusiasm and passion that you poured into your magnet, it doesn't work. It's disappointing and sometimes bewildering, because it seemed like such a good idea at the time.

As I said, I've got my own versions of that scenario that have played out in my career. Years ago I launched an entirely new division of my business that featured me, paired up with a business expert, to do two-man presentations on popular business topics to corporate events and meetings.

I thought I had properly scoped out the potential market simply by asking friends in the business who would be typical buyers of the concept. The problem is, they were my friends, and thus inclined to say nice things and be enthusiastic about my new idea. When I took the idea public and waited for the orders to roll in, I was met with resounding silence from the marketplace.

It had seemed like such a good idea. I thought it was the greatest idea since roller coasters. Turns out that I was pretty much the only person who thought it was a good idea. So, back to the drawing board.

That's all part of the process, and I can promise you that I'll have more ideas that won't work. But there's a lesson that applies to any of us looking at new business ideas or to expand our services, product lines, etc. A magnet needs a market, and we have to get clarity on that part of the business equation in order to give our new ideas a fighting chance to succeed.

Who's Going to Pay You for It?

To have a viable business you have to have people who want to buy what you're selling. Seems pretty obvious, doesn't it? It's like the ultimate "duh." Countless businesses fail because someone came up with what seemed to be a great idea but never identified the real world market for it.

When debating the pros and cons of starting a new venture, expanding a business's offerings, adding products, etc., I have sometimes been accused of being a bit of a Grinch. I plead guilty, because I'm usually the first person to ask the question, "Who's going to buy this?" "Who will actually give you money for this?" and "How are you going to reach those people who might possibly buy this?"

Spreadsheets Don't Buy Anything. (Friends Usually Don't, Either.)

Famous last words: "I've run the numbers, and if we only sell 300 of these a month, we'll make a profit. If we sell 500, we are solid gold!"

I know people who spend more time playing with spread-sheet dreams of what they imagine and hope will be than they do on the viability of whatever it is they want to sell. It's so easy to fall into the trap of encouragement by friends who have no skin in the game whatsoever. "It's a sure thing!" "You are going to get rich with this!" "This is a goldmine!" Then you start doing the math and spending your money before you've sold a thing.

Famous last words of a failed business: "But everybody loved the idea."

Worthless. Worse than worthless. It's dangerous to try and launch, build, or change a business based on you and your coworkers, your friends, or theoretical, would-be customers all loving the idea without seriously researching and understanding if people will go beyond the love and get to the money.

To succeed, you must have absolute clarity on who will willingly give you their money and how you will reach them. Until you've figured that out, you don't have a business, you only have an idea. Ideas are fine on their own, but at some point someone's got to buy something, or your idea is simply a hobby. Who is your customer, and how do you get to them?

A Great Idea in the Wrong Market

A few years ago I was asked to invest in a startup company that would be a bricks and mortar grocery store as well as offer online ordering with home delivery. The proposed location was great, the upscale concept was great, and the management team was great. It was a great idea, and I believed there was a market for it, especially given the location of the store. I was all in.

But then the plan changed. Instead of having a physical store, it became just an online grocery with home delivery. The founding partner made a case that a grocery home delivery business alone would be a hit in Nashville.

It might have been a great idea for other markets, but in Nashville I didn't feel there was a market for it. In San Francisco, Chicago, or Cincinnati, maybe a good idea with a market. But not here. Not yet. My feeling was that Nashville simply wasn't "urban" enough to support a home delivery grocery business, because Nashville is very much a "get in your car and go" town. It's not yet a "bring it to me" town, not even in the downtown area.

The team pressed on, started the business (without me as an investor) and, after a valiant effort of about a year, closed the delivery doors and called it a day. Two of the three original aspects of the business had still been valid—that the upscale concept was great and that the management team was great. But one aspect, home delivery, wasn't great. I still believe that it would have worked with a physical store in the proposed location. But it ended up being a good idea in the wrong place.

Just Follow Your Passion. If . . .

I hear it all the time. "Follow your passion and the money will come." Okay. That can be true, as long as you are really, really good at doing whatever your passion is, and as long as there are people willing and able to pay you to do it. If your passion is building very expensive, ultra-quality, craftsman guitars, as it is for my friend Alan, there'd better be people willing to pay the high price he charges. Happily for Alan, there are. But just because you love to do it doesn't mean anyone's willing to pay you to do it. A magnet needs a market.

There are other factors to consider, as well. After you've identified your market both in terms of who your potential customers are and where they are, you have to know who else is in the same space selling the same thing.

In my grocery home delivery business example, I offer San Francisco as a better location for that kind of business. But in San Francisco a cursory search online turns up Safeway, Mollie Stone's, Instacart, Google Shopping Express, Good Eggs, Amazon Fresh, Envoy, Red Sea Market, and the list goes on and on of grocery companies that deliver. Is the market too saturated to support a new magnet in town? It's a question that has to be answered.

"I'll Put It on the Internet."

It's a phrase that I feel as if I hear almost daily from someone who has an idea for a business: "I'll put it on the Internet." I am flabbergasted by the number of seemingly reasonable, intelligent people who think that all they have to do is put their product or service "on the Internet" and then just wait for the money to roll in.

Recently, I had lunch with a good friend who is a brilliant business consultant and coach with a great training program, a new book to launch, plans for speaking at meetings and events, and a new webinar series. She had asked for my thoughts and advice on her venture, so I began with a series of questions that we used as a basis for our discussion:

"Who is your market? Is it individuals or is it businesses?"

"Is what you do about personal growth or business growth?"

"Is the purpose of the book to get you coaching business, speaking business, and/or webinar business? Or are all of those businesses designed to help you sell more books? Or is it both?"

"Who is your target market for speaking? Corporations, associations, small businesses, business owners, entrepreneurs?"

"If your hope is to sell thousands of copies of the book to individuals, how will they know that it exists?"

"How will corporate meeting planners and potential coaching clients know that you exist?"

"What will differentiate your coaching, speaking, and book from the multitude of other choices out there?"

"Why is your price, whatever it may be, better than the prevailing price of similar resources on the Internet, which is 'free'?"

"How do you offer more value at your price than everything on youtube.com and TED.com, which is all free?"

"What do you really want to do? What do you love doing the most?"

The questions went on and on with our ultimate goal being to help her get clarity on exactly who her market is and how she will win in that market. Her answer to many of my questions was some version of "I'll put it on the Internet" or "I've got a company that's going to 'push it out there' for me." She was counting on success with the book "once it gets online."

This particular entrepreneur is smart enough to figure it out, and I have no doubt that she will. What's really smart is that she is willing to ask herself those very tough questions before launching a business based only on hope and wishful thinking.

The Most Crowded Market in the Universe

The opportunity of the Internet is that everyone buying anything goes there, whether it's in the consumer arena or business to business. The great and almost incomprehensible challenge of the Internet is that everyone is also on there trying to sell something. It is the most crowded market in the universe.

I had a friend who was launching a video training program online. He said, "Joe, all I need is 100 people to sign up each month and I'm gold!" My response was, "How in the world are you going to get 100 people a month to sign up for this?"

His thinking was that you can put anything on the Internet and enough people will buy it to make your business viable.

Sorry. Rarely is that the case.

If your magnetism strategy for attracting business is to do it on the Internet, then you need to have something working for you to make that a feasible place for you to set up shop. You've got to have clarity on how you'll get to that potential market you're going for. Some of the obvious factors in your favor might include:

- Having a platform of existing customers who already follow you online.
- Partnering with some entity that has existing customers they will share with you.
- Powerful search engine optimization (SEO).
- Effective social media that drives business to you.
- Using PR and align with bloggers.
- Advertising.

Any or all of these can help make your Internet business work, but there are a thousand other factors that come into play. All of them are much easier said than done, and even doing them might not create anywhere near the results that you need.

Take social media, for example. I hear people say, "I've got to get something up on social media. Maybe I should tweet. That will get some business coming my way."

Really? I mean, seriously? That's your strategy?

The subject of doing business on the Internet is worth an entire book on its own, and there are multitudes out there to choose from. Regardless of whether your marketplace is the Internet, a specific customer-targeted niche, or your neighborhood, you have to not only get clarity on who your market is, but keep on refining that clarity as your market changes (see the chapter Who Moved My Market?).

- Who, exactly, is your market?
- Who is going to willingly and eagerly pay you for this product or service?
- What makes you so sure they will do that?
- What makes you think they want this product or service?
- How will potential customers know that your new product, service, or business exists?
- Who else is offering this product or service, and what will differentiate you from them?
- What are the three things that you will get right every single time with this product or service that will cause your customers to drive new customers to you with positive word of mouth?

13

Lessons from a Startup Magnet

Looking at Your Business with New Eyes

What can we learn from a startup company that's working to become magnetic? How can we look at our own businesses with new eyes by looking through the eyes of a new entrepreneur? How can someone like me, who's been in business for over 30 years, benefit from the experience of someone well over 30 years younger than me who's just starting out?

Read on because this interview with Nick Gilson has insights, ideas, and wisdom that can help any of us look at what we do with new eyes. Imagine the challenge, excitement, and freedom of starting a business and being able to do it in any way you choose. The truth is that most of us are in a position to rethink and reinvent much more than we might imagine. Let this case study about a brand new snowboard manufacturing company and its founder's vision serve to inspire you to imagine what can be with your own business.

David and Goliath

I'm playing a small role as investor and advisor with a new company called Gilson Boards. Gilson is an American snowboarding company that designs bases in three dimensions for an enhanced feel on the mountain. From their website, here's their story:

> The team is a close group of designers, craftsmen, and adventurers. We come from different backgrounds, but we share one thing—we love what we do.
>
> We believe in the value of American artisan manufacturing, which is why we build our boards with locally grown trees here in central Pennsylvania.

We merge the woodworking heritage of our region with the precision of modern technology, building snowboards that are of the highest quality in construction.

What this little American company brings to market is the first true innovation in snowboard design. Again, from their website:

Our bases take advantage of a relatively simple concept—in motion, snow behaves much like water and air. Like airplanes and boats, our snowboards are intentionally curved to deliver a better ride.

The stark reality is that Gilson is much like David, facing the Goliaths of the snowboarding companies that have been around forever and that currently command the lion's share of the market. The challenge is for the new guy, the little guy, to take on the big guys and beat them. How do you do it? How do you create a magnet strong enough to win enough market share to take hold, grow, and thrive as a business?

Lessons for All of Us

In talking with Nick Gilson about this company he leads, I discovered lessons for all of us, whether you are a 100-year-old bank, a chiropractor with a solo practice, a plumbing-supplies distributor, or any other kind of business. Pay attention to Nick's thinking and strategies. Whether you agree or disagree with his ideas, my hope is that they will serve as a catalyst for you to consider what course you'd take with your business if you were starting over today. By the way, we all start over every day.

Joe: Where did the idea for Gilson Boards come from?

Nick: Gilson Boards grew out of a small basement crawl-space in Nashville, Tennessee. At the time, Austin Royer and I were science teachers at New Vision Academy, and we had a real focus on hands-on learning. We had this idea for three-dimensional base snowboard design—basically borrowing the fluid dynamics concepts from boats and planes and adapting them for snow. Up until that point, all snowboards and skis were flat on the bottom.

Joe: You've said that being teachers and working with those kids was actually a factor in how you were able to bounce back from an initial failure.

Nick: We were developing these concepts outside of school, but we were involving the kids in what became a sort-of yearlong lab experiment. We wanted to put our money where our mouth was and show the kids what it meant to be a curious person devoted to lifelong learning. In the process, we inadvertently demonstrated what total rock-bottom failure looks like, and the kids were really the inspiration to pick ourselves back up and hit the drawing boards again.

I honestly think we would have tossed in the towel if we hadn't had their watchful eyes on us. We knew we couldn't teach them to give up; we had to learn from the failure and demonstrate persistence.

Joe: Ultimately, you hit on a design for the snowboard that worked and that was the crossroads that ultimately drive the decision to create the company, correct?

Nick: After a number of failed experiments, we hit a variation on the snowboard design that showed tons of potential—it was both quantitatively faster and quali-tatively more fun to ride. It was a tough transition, but the kids were really invested in the project, and at the end of the year we had this emotionally charged conversation where they ultimately decided that we had to pursue this idea, even though it meant leaving each other at the end of the school year.

Joe: For people wanting a case study of how to begin a business from humble beginnings, Gilson Boards almost sounds like a made-up story. You literally started the business in a stable, is that right?

Nick: We then moved to Pennsylvania where Austin grew up, and we started developing a product and process out of a donkey stable while we were living in a cabin that had no running water or electricity. Those days were totally awesome.

Joe: You've said that a key to your success thus far is that you took the product straight to the market. This is where your own "magnetism" as a company began.

Nick: We've successfully toured the most stunning mountains in the United States every winter and experienced high growth in sales and production ability. The public's perception of our designs has shifted from "that's crazy" to "wow, this is a better way to ride." We now have a community of riders that swear by our work and vow to never ride another board until the day they die. Every time we hear that, it is like drinking 20 cups of coffee—so motivating.

Joe: So where is Gilson Boards today? Do you have any sense that you're "there" yet, or do you still have a long way to go?

Nick: Today, we're a team of 10 people, we operate a 5,000-plus-square-foot manufacturing facility in central

Pennsylvania, and we still send members of the core team out on a national tour every winter. It's been an exciting ride so far, but as a company we're still incredibly young, and there are countless variables ahead, as always.

Joe: You're starting a new business in a market that's dominated by really well-established companies. How can you expect to compete?

Nick: That is a great question, Joe. Our industry is young, and we've identified an opportunity that we're capitalizing on.

Snowboarding was born out of a juxtaposition to skiing, and that counterculture mentality of "F-the-man" fostered the industry's exponential growth for a long time. Snowboarding was growing faster than skiing by a tremendous amount for many, many years, and then the growth just totally flatlined.

Joe: So you've got a market with flat growth. How do you take on that challenge?

Nick: So what happened? The counterculture kids are now having kids. The demographic is maturing, but the messaging is staying the same. Almost every other snowboard company is competing in the crazy tricks space, with advertisements showing double back flips off of buildings into flat parking lots. That is not how most snowboarders ride—maybe 2 percent of them at the most. They don't resonate with that messaging.

Most snowboarders head out with their group or family for a fun day on the mountain, and by the way, most of those groups have skiers in them, too. Most snowboarders don't hate skiers, so why is the ad media telling us we should?

The snowboarding media says it's cool to hate skiers and that there are "no friends on a powder day." I have given my skier friends the best powder lines too many times to count, and they have done the same for me, and we always wait for each other at the bottom.

Joe: So you're painting a picture for the marketplace that runs counter to what the mainline snowboard manufacturers have painted for years?

Nick: I cannot believe that other manufacturers don't see it, or at least don't accept it. I guess it's sort of like being in a bad relationship, though; you don't really know how bad it is until it's over, despite what all your friends (read: the data) tell you. These other manufactures have watched their industry's growth flatten, and they just keep doing the same thing figuring it worked before.

Joe: And you see this as an opportunity.

Nick: At Gilson we love this. It gives us our opportunity, and we're capitalizing.

Joe: So what's the new message to your target market?

Nick: We're pioneering a new twofold message: 1. There is a better way to design snowboards that enhances your feel on the mountain, and 2. You don't have to do flips and tricks to be cool in our community. Our community is made up of park riders, young kids, older riders, carvers, college kids, families, and yes, skiers. You are welcome in our community if you love being outside, and being cool isn't just about how good you are at riding, it's about who you are as a person.

The response to this new line of thinking in the industry has been inspiring. Snowboarding as a sport isn't flattening, it is maturing, and we are positioning ourselves to be at the forefront of that maturation.

Joe: What have you done that has really worked well thus far?

Nick: Our national tours have really worked the way we've wanted them to. I think more than anything, people are searching for authenticity when purchasing luxury products. The story matters, and our story resonates with people.

Joe: You seem to be a combination of a cutting-edge kind of company, with a new product and a new marketing message, and yet you are, in many ways, an old school manufacturing company.

Nick: We're not a software startup raising millions before our first dollar of revenue. We're an American manufacturing company. We build our products ourselves, and then we tour the country ourselves. We don't outsource our manufacturing, and we don't hire reps to promote our products. Yes, we use the Internet and social media— we are a modern and technologically advanced company, but down to the roots we have a traditional structure, and people really miss that.

We're described as being an earnest and respectful group that has pulled themselves up by their bootstraps, and that means something to people. Our story matters to people. When you're buying toilet paper, who cares? You just get the nicest or cheapest kind. The story doesn't matter. But when you're buying a snowboard—a product that you will develop a relationship with and likely personify—it's no longer just about price. Who made your board matters, and where they made it matters. The whole story matters.

Joe: Taking your boards out to the mountains and getting face-to-face with your potential customers has been an important part of mix for you, hasn't it?

Nick: The tour serves as a wonderful first point of contact with the company. Our people forgo running water and warmth to meet great people and find the best snow. We immerse ourselves in our community, and that allows us to listen and learn an awful lot about how we can support our riders and our retailers.

Whether you interact with our tour in person or online, it really does give you a good idea of what we value as a company and who we are.

Joe: What are a couple of valuable lessons that you've learned so far?

Nick: The most significant lesson I've learned is that failure is hugely important, and it should be treasured. Don't waste failures. Do it quickly and often. Failure is when you learn the most, and that experience should be squeezed for every last drop of insight every time it happens. A success is either an accident (we've had a few of those), or it is the culmination of all the lessons learned during repeated failures.

Joe: A lot of people believe that their success or failure is all about the idea. You've got a new, unique idea with Gilson Boards. Is your success all about that idea?

Nick: I've learned that a good idea accounts for less than 1 percent of what it takes to bring a new product to market, and along the same vein, surrounding yourself with a team of highly intelligent and persistent people is crucial. Persistence is the keyword there, given that you're going to need to fail a lot in order to succeed, and it is much more fun if there is no loss in enthusiasm.

Joe: You and I tend to agree on the idea that less truly can be more, and that simplifying your business can be a competitive advantage.

Nick: I've learned that building a business is a lot like writing an excellent essay—the delete key is one of the most important buttons. It's okay to start with 10 pages, but if you really want to make it great, figure out how to convey the same message and emotion in one page. There are certain risks you will take when building a business, and sometimes you need to stick to your guns against all odds, and at other times you need to be able to shift course quickly, even if it means deleting a few sentences you thought sounded great.

Joe: As the company grows, what do you look for in new employees?

Nick: We look for two mind-sets in particular when hiring: perseverance and intelligence. Smart people who are also persistent can do just about anything if given the resources. Our business operations guy, Steve Blackman, is also our accountant, and he was trained as a journalist. He's smart, and he works outrageously hard. When he fails, he yells a little, but then he pulls himself up by his bootstraps and figures it out. His training means almost nothing compared to his way of thinking.

Joe: One of the things I have found in over 30 years of working with and studying successful businesses is that what's most important is mind-set. Strategies and tactics vary wildly from business to business, but the truly successful ones seem to share some common threads when it comes to the mind-set of the people who work there. Talk about that mind-set of perseverance and intelligence that you look for.

Nick: Being wrong and persistent gets you to a bad place. Being right with no persistence gets you nowhere. Being right and persistent is how you get the job done. Intelligent people find the right answer most of the time. Persistent people get the job done, regardless of unforeseen obstacles. Intelligent and persistent people grow successful businesses and realize their goals.

Joe: In a new business like yours, how important is the teamwork factor?

Nick: All this said about individual mind-set, we also attempt to measure how well a potential hire will mesh with the team. We had a dream candidate apply recently. He was smarter and more educated than me by a factor of 10, no question. He was clearly persistent, but he had trouble listening when others were talking. It was subtle, but over time that is a recipe for disaster on a small team. We had to pass on the opportunity. I would have made the wrong decision a few years ago.

Joe: What do you think will be your biggest challenges going forward?

Nick: We have two primary challenges moving forward. We operate in a seasonal market, and we offer a made-to-order, customizable product—and yes, those two challenges are related. Snowboards are primarily purchased between August and January. Last year, our build team was working 80 to 100 hours per week during those months. In June, they were off the clock and building a board here and there over a beer. We could stock inventory, but we're a young company, and we don't have enough data to make those decisions and still be able to sleep at night. What if we spend the summer stocking the wrong inventory? That could kill us. Perhaps more important, inventory takes away from the feeling people get when purchasing a board from Gilson. We make each board for an individual, even if it is one of our standard models. Your board isn't waiting for you on a warehouse shelf. Your board doesn't even exist yet, but it will be on your doorstep in a week if you click that button. There is something special about that.

Joe: It sounds like part of the challenge for you might be growth in orders, which is what you want, but it's also what can kill you if you don't manage it properly.

Nick: As we grow, we have to be increasingly intelligent about how we approach production and seasonal variability. We don't have the wiggle room to misstep, and we need to maintain our intensely high-quality standards in production, which is really hard to do when orders are growing exponentially. We're not going to sacrifice our artisan philosophy to sell lower-quality boards for a few extra bucks on the bottom line. We care too much about our company, and we care too much about your ride. We would rather tell people that they can't get a board at the moment, which is always a sad thing for us to do.

Joe: What do you consider to be the company's greatest strengths?

Nick: This is the hardest question you've asked so far. I cannot tell you how many manufacturing and business folks have walked into our facility and had their jaws drop—talking about the "continuous improvement mind-sets" and the "innovation at work" and how we're "doing all the things they teach by the seat of our pants." We hear it every day, which is nice I suppose, but none of us see it. Ask any member of the team what's on their mind and odds are it's something going wrong. We see future problems far more clearly than we see historical successes. I'm told that is in itself a strength, but it isn't making us any younger, that's for sure.

Joe: On the face of it, the fact that you go on tour every winter and get out there in the middle of your market seems like it would have to be a strength for you. I constantly encourage my clients to know more about the customer than the competition knows, and how that can be their greatest competitive advantage.

Nick: I would have to say that one of our strengths is our desire to immerse ourselves in our community and listen. We've learned so much on the road that we've later been able to implement back home in our facility.

Joe: I remember when you asked me what would be the first thing I'd do if I were starting the company, not as a 26-year-old, but at my age. I told you that I'd immediately hire some 26-year-olds. What are the ups and downs of starting a business with such a young team?

Nick: We are a young team, and that comes with its own set of challenges, but we've found that inexperience can also be an asset. We've had a number of internal inventions that allow us to build better snowboards, but we never would have found those solutions if we had known the "standard" way of doing things. A number of years ago, all the world's most knowledgeable academics and scientists knew that human flight would never be achieved.

What If I Were Starting Over?

Being a part of this new company has been mentally invigorating for me in terms of how I think about my own business. It's intriguing to any of us who have been in business for a long time to think in terms of: "What if I were starting all over? If I were building this business from scratch, what would I do differently? What would I change?"

Nick and his team at Gilson Boards are doing just that—starting a company from scratch and building it exactly the way they want to. Some of what they do will work. Some of it won't. The journey from having a glorious idea to having a company that makes a profit is a long, complicated walk.

Most of the people who read this book will probably also agree that the journey from having a profitable company to sustaining that success is also a complicated walk, and it requires a combination of continuous vigilance, openness to change, and as Nick pointed out, never-ending persistence.

- If I were starting my business today, what would I do differently?
- What am I willing to do right now to move my business toward that ideal "new beginnings" state of being?

(continued)

(*continued*)

- Do I need to be more resilient in the face of setbacks?
- How can we do a better job of directly connecting with our customers and target market community? How can we learn more about what they like, don't like, want, and need?
- Could we benefit by redefining the beliefs and assumptions about our market or business like Gilson Boards is doing?
- Do we squeeze "every drop of insight" from our failures?
- How can we simplify our business? What should we "delete" from the way we do business?
- What mind-set do we look for in our employees? Have we even thought about that enough?
- What are our biggest challenges? How will we overcome them?
- What are we greatest strengths? Do we truly leverage them to the greatest extent possible? How can we get even better at those things that we already do extremely well?

14

Who Moved My Market?

Whom Would You Call?

Triumph International is a German lingerie manufacturing business. They wanted to sell bras online. Who did they call to make that happen? Well, of course they called whom any of us would call in that situation. They called the 200-year-old national postal service of Singapore.

Just as Triumph International was changing their business to meet the changing demands of their marketplace, Singapore Post had also changed their business to stay relevant in a marketplace that had gone from letters, postcards, and stamps to e-communication and e-commerce.

We all have to remagnetize.

Your market is changing. You may think your market is evolving slowly, with plenty of time for you to make adjustments and small changes as you go along. But the chances are that your market is changing, or about to change, much more rapidly than you imagine. You'd better be prepared to move quickly on to your "next act."

It's become almost a tired old cliché to say that everything from customers to technology to society and the entire world is constantly and rapidly changing. Sadly, many businesses will intellectually acknowledge that change but then go back to doing business like they've always done it, as if somehow they were operating in a vacuum in which either change wasn't taking place, or that the changes that were happening would affect everyone but them.

Some of us are old enough to remember playing with old-fashioned horseshoe-shaped magnets when we were kids. Sooner or later those magnets would lose their ability to attract metal objects. They would literally become demagnetized. You either had to throw the magnet away or find a way to remagnetize it.

The simplest way to remagnetize was to rub a strong magnet repeatedly in one direction along the weak magnet.

Remagnetizing a business is anything but simple. No business escapes the need to change. We all face the danger of becoming irrelevant unless we stay one step ahead of changes like decreasing demand, shifts in customer wants and needs, or increased and sometimes unexpected competition.

The Opportunity of a Burning Platform

The phrase "burning platform" has become entrenched in popular business jargon these days. Generally it means any crisis situation that forces a business to either change or perish. The origin of the phrase is said to be in a story of an oil worker on a rig in the North Sea. The rig catches fire, and the worker is faced with either a fiery death or jumping from the burning platform into an icy sea. He jumps, the story goes, and is rescued by a boat.

I use burning platform to describe the increasingly common business reality that the demand for what you do, in the way you've always done it, is disappearing. It may be a slow erosion of demand or might be happening quickly, but it can happen to any of us and is, in fact, happening to most of us.

It's not being naive or unrealistically optimistic to suggest that the reasonable response to a burning platform is to find the next opportunity and go there. That's what Singapore Post has done, along with many others who took their next big step and are doing quite well, thank you. I believe that any business can learn practical, immediately usable lessons from their example.

We Print Checks. Now What?

For many years I had the privilege of doing work with Deluxe Corp. To this day they remain one of my favorite clients, and they are a great example of a company that has found opportunity in what many would call a burning platform.

For years, Deluxe did pretty much one thing: They printed checks for bank customers. If you use checks, chances are that you have Deluxe checks in your purse, back pocket, or desk drawer right now. Deluxe was, and still is, a great innovator in the check business, and they have developed great relationships with the banks and credit unions whose customers they serve.

While Deluxe still does quite well in the check business, there's no doubt that checks are, little by little, being replaced by debit cards and direct online payments. As this trend became more obvious, Deluxe had to determine what their next step would be.

Taking into consideration their core capabilities, the strengths of their people, and trends in the marketplace, Deluxe saw opportunity in expanding beyond just helping banks and credit unions grow and into helping a range of businesses grow by providing a range of services.

Today, Deluxe Corp. provides checks, forms, marketing solutions, accessories, and other products and services for small businesses and financial institutions.

This isn't rocket science. The lesson for you and for me is to take stock in yourself, your strengths, and your possibilities, and match those with a clear-headed assessment of the marketplace. It's no time for wishful thinking or clinging to any notion that "the market will always come to us" when all evidence is to the contrary. Instead of waiting for your traditional market to come to you, now may be the time to get in front of the new market reality and begin to attract that business.

Who Moved My Market?

A few years ago there was a very popular business book called *Who Moved My Cheese?* that dealt with how to effectively deal with change. Today the change that most of us have to deal with on an ever-increasing basis is "who moved my market?"

You can be the leader in your market, lose touch for what seems like the blink of an eye, and the next thing you know, you've become irrelevant, your magnetism is lost, and your customers are disappearing.

Let's look at two areas of business that are experiencing markets on the move. The first is the fast food or casual dining restaurant business. That used to be a market driven by speed (I want it fast) and taste (I want it good).

That market has moved.

Today customers of fast food and casual dining restaurants want, as reported by *Money* magazine, "customizable options, transparency, and fare that's healthier, more sustainable, and altogether superior compared to any cheap cookie-cutter fast food joint." They are leaving icons like McDonald's and Subway in favor of what they consider to be smarter choices like Chipotle Mexican Grill and Panera Bread.

Subway is responding by taking actions such as dropping all artificial ingredients from their menu. Panera Bread saw the same shift and took out a full-page ad in *USA Today* with an open letter from Panera founder, Chairman, and CEO Ron Shaich, which opened with "Dear America." In the letter Shaich promised that "no other company is moving as aggressively to offer clean food. We want to encourage suppliers and competitors to rethink the way that they do business, too. We want to set an example for the change our food system so desperately needs."

I would suggest to you that your market has moved, is moving today, and will continue to move tomorrow. How? Where? That's what you have to find out. Every market is different.

My second example of a moving market is my business, which is the business of professionals who do consulting and speaking to business groups at corporate events and conventions. Somebody has moved my market.

Speaker magazine is a publication of the National Speakers Association. CEO Stacy Tetschner surveyed a group of seasoned professional speakers about recent changes in that market. Here are some of the changes they see as reported in *Speaker* magazine:

- Many groups no longer hire "traditional" speakers. They hire book experts, interesting people, entrepreneurs, bloggers, adventurers, athletes, and celebrities.
- TED Talks have changed how many planners are viewing and hiring speakers. Audiences prefer shorter presentations by people not normally thought of as being professional speakers.
- Audiences are savvier and more active in sharing their opinions about speakers. They are actively using social media and various rating systems. (There's that customer word of mouth!)
- There is a greater supply than demand, with price competitiveness and commoditization.
- The odds of being displaced by newer, hotter, hipper, and trendier speakers are higher than ever.

The market in my business hasn't just moved; for some of my colleagues it has virtually disappeared because of all the changes.

The position that you may have owned at one time in your market may have literally disappeared. Many businesses make the mistake of trying to convince the old market to come back, rather than reading the writing on the wall and changing to get ahead of where the market is going.

Movements in my market have driven some significant and fundamental changes in the way I do business and in how I define my value proposition. Quite frankly, I see the changes as an opportunity to differentiate. And even more frankly, what choice do I have? I either use moves in the market to create opportunity or I hang a "closed" sign on my door and find something else to do.

We Live in Interesting Times

In June 1966, Robert Kennedy gave a speech in which he said, "There is a Chinese curse which says, 'May you live in interesting times.' Like it or not, we live in interesting times. They are times of danger and uncertainty; but they are also more open to the creative energy of men than any other time in history."

Some quick Internet research reveals that, in truth, that "Chinese curse" has no connection to China or Chinese culture whatsoever. It's also interesting these days to see a reference to "the creative energy of men." I'm pretty sure there were women with creative energy around in 1966. But I digress.

Whatever business you are in, you most definitely live in interesting times. We are all our own version of Singapore Post, which faced a changing or disappearing market. We will either be able to transition successfully as our markets move and change, or we will find ourselves wondering where all the customers went.

- Where are the movements in our market?
- How are we responding to them?
- Where will the next moves be, and will we be there safely ahead of the changes?
- How will we have to be different in five years? In three?
- What single change in the marketplace has the greatest potential to put us out of business?
- What will we do to stay viable?

15
You're Fired!

The Common (and Fatal) Mistakes That Businesses Make

I cowrote a blog called *The Five Friends* with my friends Larry Winget, Mark Sanborn, Randy Pennington, and Scott McKain. In the blog, we talk about subjects ranging from the greatest challenges that businesses face and best practices for employers to how selling has changed and the relative importance of hiring vs. training. We cover a lot of ground, and occasionally we use the blog to just let off some steam about things that are bothering us. Recently, our blog dealt with the common (and fatal) mistakes that businesses make and, specifically, businesses that each of us have fired as a result.

It can take years to build your magnetism with customers, and it can be lost in an instant. Often we lose a customer because of simple and completely avoidable mistakes. The great danger is that we might lose our vigilance against making such mistakes and lose customers because we simply weren't paying attention.

What follows are our stories of companies we have fired and the reasons we did.

I'll begin with my own contribution to the "You're Fired!" blog with my story about six infuriating months I spent in a quagmire of off-the-charts terrible customer service at the hands of the phone company.

Joe Calloway Fired a Phone Company

A couple of years ago I fired a company that had become irrelevant to me, and the ensuing madness and incompetence was almost beyond description. I will never do business with them again. I had a telephone line for my office—a land line that

I almost never used. Finally I pulled the plug, cancelled the service, and that was that. Not.

For six months I dealt with the phone company reps who threatened me with collection agency action for my unpaid bill—on a line I had cancelled months earlier. One rep would say, "Oh, you cancelled that line. Don't worry. I'll take care of it." The next week I'd get a letter from their legal department saying, "You're delinquent on your bill—we're suing." Back and forth, to and fro, one rep more incompetent and uncaring than the next.

I think the two big, common mistakes that this company made were (1) having a system in which one department had no idea what another was doing, and (2) hiring people who simply didn't care about the customer.

I guess if I were to boil it down even more, I'd say to this company: "Don't be incompetent. Don't be mean. Don't be stupid."

Mark Sanborn Fired a Restaurant

How do you go from being one of a customer's favorite companies to being fired by that same customer? I'd love to tell you that it's a difficult thing to do, but the truth is that it's easy. Mark Sanborn is president of Sanborn & Associates, Inc., an idea studio for leadership development. He is an award-winning speaker and the bestselling author of books including *The Fred Factor*, one of the best books ever written about customer service. Here's the story from Mark Sanborn of a restaurant that went from "favorite" to "fired."

I fired one of my favorite restaurant chains. As much as I enjoyed eating there, I reached a point where "enough was enough." Most interestingly, it was triggered when I tried to give management some positive feedback.

I took my family to a local seafood chain restaurant to celebrate a birthday. The experience was a parody of what should have happened: slow service, wrong drink orders, wrong food orders, and more. It was exasperating and, since I was hosting relatives, a bit embarrassing.

A young manager, however, saved the day. She apologized sincerely, comped the entire meal, and provided me a $50 gift certificate to encourage me to return.

I tried to compliment her to corporate. The website feedback form was convoluted, but I filled in the required information and praised the assistant manager. The promised "response within 48 hours" never came.

I called corporate to follow up. Whoever I spoke to wasn't very helpful, so I asked for a manager to call me. She said she'd have someone call but started to hang up the phone before she got my phone number!

At least she did pass on the information to someone as the local restaurant manager called a few days later and left a message. He said he'd be out of town on a trip and would follow up when he returned. He never did.

When I tried to use the $50 certificate, I found unexpected restrictions. I expressed my frustration to my server but got not even a little empathy in return.

It was the final straw.

At the time I was writing a *Five Friends* blog about our favorite restaurants. One of the categories was "favorite chain restaurant." I had planned to use this particular one, but could no longer do so in good conscience so dropped them from the list.

All customers have a threshold that, once crossed, destroys loyalty. It takes surprisingly little time or effort to acknowledge and appreciate a customer who provides positive or negative feedback. Ignoring such feedback or taking it lightly can cause a customer to fire you.

Larry Winget Fired the Garage Door Company, the Air Conditioning Company, and His Doctor

My friend Larry Winget tells it like it is. He doesn't mince words, and he says exactly what he means. Larry is known as the Pitbull of Personal Development, and he is a six-time *New York Times* and *Wall Street Journal* bestselling author, a social commentator, and appears regularly on many national television news shows.

Here's Larry's story about who he fired and why:

My motto for life and business: Do what you said you would do, when you said you would do it, the way you said you would do it. If you don't, you're a liar and we won't work together.

I wanted some new garage doors, so I contacted what was advertised to be the best company in town. They had big ads in all of the fancy home magazines and had exactly the door I was looking for, so I called and we set the appointment. When the day and time of the appointment came, the company representative didn't show up and didn't bother to call to let me know why. I called him, as I had his cell phone number from when he set the appointment, and he didn't answer his phone so I left a voice mail. When he got to my house four hours later with no apology and no explanation of why he was late, I explained to him that not showing up on time and not calling me the instant he knew he was going to be late was disrespectful of my time and that we wouldn't be doing business. He was amazed that I felt that way, saying that he got delayed on a previous job and that it had nothing to do with disrespecting me. I told him that if he couldn't keep his word about an appointment, then I couldn't trust his doors, his price quote, or his promised delivery date, and that I had already contacted another company. He left not understanding any of it.

I had a problem with my air conditioner and hired a company to come check out the problem. They worked on it and explained that I would probably need to buy a new one. I was prepared for that and told them to get me a bid. However, when I went out later to look at my air conditioner after they were long gone, I discovered food wrappers, paper cups and wire clippings all around the unit. I called and told them not to bother with a bid. These guys missed the sale of a new air conditioner all because they didn't take 15 seconds to clean up after themselves. Again, a matter of disrespect of me and my property.

I visited my doctor for a checkup. After sitting in the waiting room for nearly an hour past my appointment time, I asked the receptionist why it had been so long and when I was going to be seen. She told me that she had no idea and that I could ask the doctor when I talked to him. I told her I would be happy to ask the doctor when I talked to him and asked again when she thought that might be. The receptionist then told me to "go sit down." I'm a grown man and don't respond well to being talked to like

I am a seven-year-old, especially when I am the customer and you are clearly in the wrong. I told her that my new doctor would be contacting them for my records as I was no longer a patient there. When I wrote the doctor about my experience, I never got a response back. This is another case where a business didn't respect my time or my business and was rude.

I am an easy guy to do business with: Respect my time, respect my business, respect the fact that you can easily be replaced as few have a complete monopoly on anything. It's really so simple.

Randy Pennington Fired the Lawn Service

Randy Pennington is one of the smartest guys I know and is a brilliant business speaker, advisor, and author. Randy helps a wide range of leaders in business, government, and nonprofits deliver positive results in a world of accelerating change.

Randy's story is one that all of us can relate to as customers, but one that hopefully you will never experience in your business with your own customers. Beware of the danger of success. In Randy's story, you see how having so much business that you can't keep up with it can cause customers to leave.

We fired the service that had done all of our lawn care, landscaping, tree trimming, and holiday lights for 17 years. There wasn't one single incident that caused us to leave. It was the culmination of a number of little things over an 18-month period.

In the beginning, the owner closely supervised the crews, paid attention to quality, and was excellent in following up and communicating. Then again, his business was new and hungry.

Over the years, the service level and responsiveness diminished. E-mails and telephone messages went unanswered for up to a week. The quality of the work became inconsistent, and we could no longer count on him to follow through on requests without constant prodding.

And yet, we weren't really looking to change. He's a good guy, and we tried to understand when he told us that he had so much business that keeping up was difficult. But we fired this provider for the same reasons that many personal relationships fail: inattention. We felt ignored and taken for granted. Someone made us feel wanted by asking for our business, and we said, "What have we got to lose?"

Scott McKain Fired The Oncologist

Scott McKain is one of the most sought-after speakers anywhere on customer distinction. Scott McKain teaches how organizations and individual professionals can create distinction in their marketplace and deliver the ultimate customer experience.

Scott's story is a sobering one, because it involves something very disappointing that happened during a most challenging time in his life. This story also shows us that there is no job or profession immune from getting fired. What's so sad about this is that any person serving other people could be so insensitive and oblivious to someone's feelings.

My wife and I were sharing with her oncologist about our just-completed weekend in Napa.

The doctor said to us, "Don't spend your time doing frivolous things like Napa. Your life will be ending soon."

I was flabbergasted—why would you not want to enjoy the time you had left?

"Sheri's situation is terminal and she will be gone soon." The doctor was talking as if my wife wasn't sitting right there in front of her.

Standing up and looking at the doctor, I said three words to her: "You are fired."

Her jaw dropped. "You can't fire me," she replied, "I'm a doctor."

"Call it whatever you want," I said, "but you will never see us again."

We found another oncologist—a wonderful, compassionate doctor—and Sheri had another three years of full living, enjoying each day.

Sometimes when we think about firing, we tend to think of the examples of retailers or service providers that are mentioned by my friends here.

Yet, when professionals at the highest level of social respect fail to exhibit empathy or place themselves on a pedestal that interferes with the experience of the customer, client, or patient—they, too, deserve to be fired.

It Wasn't the Lack of a "Wow" Factor

Notice something interesting about each of our stories. None of us were lured away as customers by someone else offering a "wow" factor. Nobody fired their business because it wasn't offering something "extra" or "special" or "above and beyond."

Each of us fired the business because it failed to deliver on something absolutely fundamental that we counted on. And that's what happens far too often. We take the basics for granted and think that, after a certain point in our success, we must look further to create competitive differentiation.

No! Customers are won and lost in the battle for who performs best at those handful of things that our customers expect. I think Larry said it best: "Do what you said you would do, when you said you would do it, the way you said you would do it." That's it. If you are the best at those three things, you are competitive. You will win.

I think that my biggest frustration in working with companies wanting to improve their performance is the constant distraction of "buzzers and bells" that they think will differentiate them. But that's not what makes you magnetic. That's not what attracts business. The lawn service that does the best job at what they said they'd do, shows up on time, has service-driven employees, and charges a fair price will win. Ditto for restaurants, telephone companies, and even medical practices.

Legendary NBA basketball great Michael Jordan warned that when you "get away from fundamentals . . . the bottom can fall out of your game, your schoolwork, your job . . . whatever you're doing."

Famous Last Words

You may read these stories of businesses that dropped the ball, missed the mark, or otherwise blew it and be thinking to yourself, "That could never happen to us." Those are famous last words spoken by countless businesses that lost focus and one day realized that their customers were all gone.

None of the businesses that my friends and I fired had bad intentions, not even the unfeeling doctor whom Scott and Sheri were dealing with. It's certainly not that the leaders in these businesses didn't know any better. My guess is that if you had described any of these service mishaps to them, they would have said that of course you can't do that and expect to stay in business. And yet they all did it.

There's an old saying that goes, "We don't get hurt by what we don't know. We get hurt by what we know and don't do." All of these businesses knew better than to do what they did. But knowing what to do is light years away from actually doing it. It's in the execution that we most often fail.

My best advice is to stay vigilant. With your team you must talk about the basics that our customers require of us and talk about it all the time. Professionals practice and focus on the fundamentals until they never get them wrong. The practice and focus never stops. Once you stop, you lose your edge on those fundamentals, and that's most often where you lose your magnetism and your customers.

- Are we guilty of making any of the mistakes that the fired companies made?
- What are we guilty of "knowing but not doing"?
- Where do we need to be more vigilant? How will we make sure that we stay vigilant?

16

Magnetic Connections

Go Retro

The goal is to stay forever in the forefront of your customers' minds and to keep their positive word of mouth working for you in ways that help you sustain and grow your success. There are two very old-school ways of connecting and reconnecting that, as technology grows as the common choice for communication, become progressively more powerful and effective.

Sometimes the most powerful way to magnetize (or remagnetize) our business is through the ways we connect with our customers. Certainly, if we want our customers to be sending a steady stream of new customers our way, we have to constantly, and appropriately, reach out to connect.

There are a thousand ways to connect digitally and electronically, and by the time this book comes out, you are probably connecting with your customers holographically. Good for you. I'm all for it. Leave no connection resource stone unturned.

But in a world of texts, e-mails, posts, and tweets, there are two ways of connecting that stand out in terms of impact, power, and effectiveness, and they both are decidedly retro:

Get face-to-face.

Send a handwritten note.

Get Face-to-Face

Many years ago there was a commercial for an airline that featured a business owner telling his employees that they were losing customers from inattention. He tells them that one of their best and oldest customers had called to tell him that the company had lost touch and that the customer felt taken for granted.

The owner went around the room, handing plane tickets to each employee, telling them they were going to go see their customers and reconnect with all of them. One of his employees asked, "Where are you going, boss?" The owner replied, "To see that old customer that called me."

It was a lovely, touching commercial that drove home the idea that there is nothing more powerful than making a personal, face-to-face connection. Do you believe truly personal connections are still that powerful in this age of texting, e-mail, LinkedIn, Twitter, and all of the electronic options we have at our fingertips? Well, please believe it, because the evidence shows that you can use it not only to remagnetize your business, but to create a distinct differentiation between you and your competition.

Make no mistake, I am the biggest fan in the world of electronic communication. My preferred method of everyday business and even personal communication is e-mail (not texting, although I do progressively more of that as time goes by). What I love about e-mail vs. phone calls is that e-mail forces the process of getting clarity on your thoughts so that you can put them in writing. Of course, the weakness of e-mail, texting, or other forms of electronic communication is the lack of emotional context.

There's no need to belabor the impact that a face-to-face encounter has in today's world of communication via screens. I'll give you two real world examples that make the obvious point.

Practice Retail Politics

As I write this book there's a mayoral race going on in Nashville. There are seven viable candidates, and the good news is that any of them would make a good mayor. There are no glaring differences in policy positions among them; most of the differences are a matter of degree. Beyond advertising, robo-calls (which we all hate), PR, and e-mails, how does a candidate in a crowded field stand out to a voter like me?

You knock on my door on a Saturday afternoon and spend 15 minutes asking what's important to us as citizens of Nashville. Then you answer any questions we might have about your positions. You take a lot of time to make that very personal face-to-face connection. That's what one candidate did, and it made a huge and very positive impression.

Before the election's over, other candidates might knock on my door and look me in the eye. I hope so. We'll see.

By the way, this particular mayoral candidate has a unique connection strategy on his campaign website. Here's his offer:

If you'd like to talk to me, all you need to do is schedule a time to have a quick call.

Here's my promise:

The call won't last more than 10 minutes.

I will give you the 30-second version of "Why I'm running."

Then, you'll be in charge. You can ask me any question, and I'll answer 100 percent honestly.

Then, I get to ask you a question. That's it.

During presidential election campaigns we often hear the phrase "retail politics." It means a political strategy or campaign style of meeting and speaking directly to as many voters as possible: *New Hampshire is a state where retail politics makes the difference.*

Every business could benefit from practicing its own version of more retail politics. Meet and speak directly with as many customers as possible. Of course, you have to determine what your version of that looks like, but it's worth the effort to figure it out.

My version of retail politics includes face-to-face connections with potential customers during the selling phase. In my business arena, companies often go through a vetting process in which a number of professionals who do what I do are under consideration for hiring. Often that process consists of a phone call and possibly the submission of written material from me and the others being considered.

If I have determined that this is business that I really want, I won't hesitate to offer to get on a plane and visit the prospect, for the sole purpose of determining whether we are a good fit. I won't say that it gets me the job 100 percent of the time, but suffice it to say that it works more than enough for it to be a regular strategy of mine.

The very fact that you are willing to spend the time and effort to seek someone out face-to-face instead of only through the Internet speaks volumes about your interest in them and your commitment to the relationship. It is, without question, one of the ultimate tiebreakers in business and one of the most magnetic things that you can do for your business.

Some will say that putting that much time into getting face-to-face with prospects is too expensive in terms of both money and time. That can certainly be true if you are selling retail and need pure volume that can only be generated by mass marketing. In my business, selling fairly big-ticket services business to business, I use face-to-face as a wildly effective and efficient way to close more business.

The Lost Art of the Handwritten Note

As electronic communication becomes more prevalent, the positive impact of a handwritten note becomes almost impossible to calculate. What used to be commonplace is now so unusual that it captures attention like no other form of communication or connection.

Earlier in the book I mentioned that I worked with a group of the top franchisees for a company, and part of our work was in sharing the most successful practices for business growth. Everyone knew who was the most successful franchisee in the room, and when it was his turn to share, there was great interest in what he would say.

"I send handwritten thank-you notes to my customers."

That was it. In his 20 years in business, the single greatest growth strategy he had employed was the consistent use of handwritten thank-you notes. He said that it had gotten him more positive feedback and was the catalyst for more repeat and referral business than any other thing, except for the foundational element of doing exceptional work for each customer.

There's not a lot to say about handwritten notes except that they work better as a way to connect than anything else (with the possible exception of face-to-face) and you can start using the strategy now. If nothing else, if you're thinking right now that you aren't going to send handwritten notes, at least be clear on why you won't do it. A waste of time? Other things you can do that will have a greater impact on creating positive experiences for customers? My guess is that you're wrong about those two objections, but it's your decision. If, however, your reason is that you think it won't work, then I don't have a "guess" that you're wrong. You're just flat wrong.

As a final thought on the power of the handwritten note, consider using them in-house with your employees and colleagues. My friend Marty Grunder, whom I often reference as one of the best and smartest business thinkers and leaders I know, had this to say about his use of the handwritten note with his employees:

"Over last 30 years I have written hundreds of thank-you notes to members of our team—thanking them for specific things they have done well—sometimes taking a picture of what they did—with the note. I send these notes to their homes so that they can share them with family and see how much I appreciate what they do."

The bottom line is that people are hungry to connect. Use that basic human need to build your business. Why on earth would you not?

- Whom do we need to get face-to-face with?
- Whom do we need to call?
- Whom do we need to send a handwritten note to?
- Who will do it?
- When will we do it?
- How will be sure that we will keep on doing it?

17

Losing Your Magnetic Mojo

Can a Magnet Lose Its Strength?

Physical magnets actually do lose a very small fraction of their magnetism over time. For most magnets, it has been shown to be less than 1 percent over a period of 10 years.

Factors that can affect a magnet's strength include heat, radiation, strong electrical currents in close proximity to the magnet, and other magnets in close proximity to the magnet.

Unfortunately, in the case of a business, magnetism can disappear at a much faster rate. It might happen slowly, but it can also happen in what seems like the blink of an eye.

We've all seen it. A business is booming, customers are happy, and all is well. Then one day there's a Closed sign on the door. What happened?

There are also lots of businesses that do well and grow for a while, then plateau and get stuck at a level of results that lets them survive, but not prosper.

Some businesses never get off the ground, and it's no surprise when they simply don't make it. But what about the ones that do have that magnetic mojo going on, they are doing well, maybe even extremely well, for a period of time, and yet somehow it all slips away from them?

Any number of things can cause a business's ability to attract and keep customers to disappear, and almost all of them are avoidable. It's not easy to stay in business these days because factors change all the time, including changes in customer demands, competition, technology, and much more. But what puts a once-successful enterprise out of business or at a level of less-than-optimum performance is usually one or more missteps that we think we'll never make, but they can happen all too easily to anyone.

The most dangerous threats to your magnetism, your ability to attract business, include a decline in product quality, the assumption that you're "just fine" at the fundamentals (a condition also known as complacency), and becoming irrelevant.

Rave Reviews. Amazing French Food

Here's a blog entry that I posted about a new restaurant that had opened in Nashville:

> Last year I read a review of a new French restaurant in Nashville. It's called Chelsea Bistro and it's just way the hell out in the middle of nowhere in a tiny community called Whites Creek. A long, fairly desolate drive. The review was noteworthy in its enthusiasm:
>
> When someone tells you there's a true French bistro—not French-inspired, not Cali-French, but really French—in Whites Creek, and it's superb, don't let your eyebrows leap up, don't draw your head back, and don't say, "Really?" Put a pleasant expression on your face and say, "That sounds wonderful." Because Chelsea Bistro is wonderful, and it is in Whites Creek.
>
> —*Nashville Scene,* 10/24/2013
>
> Two weeks later, another review in another publication—same thing. Truly a classic rave review.
>
> So I went. My book publisher was visiting from New York and we made the long, dark drive out of town. We found Chelsea Bistro as one of four tenants of a tiny, crappy looking little strip mall. Our initial reaction was, "You've got to be kidding me."
>
> After the appetizer (get the clams), our reaction was (in the popular vernacular) . . . "OMG!" The food was off the hook. Excellent. Even approaching amazing. I loved it.

Since that first visit, I've been back. And back again. And back again. Believe me, it's an effort. "Convenient location" this is not. The ambience is just okay, at best. The service is really good, but there aren't any cute "extras" or contrived "wow" factors.

The staff and managers are charming. The cocktails are original and excellent. Wine list—small but good.

Here's the deal, and here's why the parking lot at that crummy little strip mall is crowded much of the time. It's just the best damn French food. . . . darn near anywhere. The two rave reviews were right. Chelsea Bistro is worth the drive.

They got the basics right—especially the quality of the food that they serve. It is excellent.

If you want people to be willing to make an effort to do business with you, it's not going to happen (at least not for long) with gimmicks, buzzers, and bells.

Novelties wear off. A classically great beef bourguignon doesn't. Be the best at what matters most.

That restaurant went out of business about year later.

Note the core observation that I made about Chelsea Bistro: They got the basics right—especially the quality of the food that they serve.

I made repeated visits to Chelsea Bistro after I wrote that blog, and the restaurant continued to be absolutely wonderful. Until it wasn't.

It's Not As Good As It Used to Be

I recall the tipping point when, having dinner there with my friend Scott McKain, who was there for the first time, he said,

"This is really good." My reply was, "You know, it's not as good as it used to be."

I have no idea what happened. Maybe they changed chefs. Maybe financial pressures forced them to use lower-quality ingredients. Maybe they just stopped paying attention.

Whatever the reason, a few weeks later, the restaurant closed.

The lesson is simple and excruciatingly obvious. You cannot let the quality of your performance on the basics slip. Not ever.

This is the danger of chasing "wow" factors. It's all well and good to want to surprise and delight your customers, but if the pursuit of "wow" causes you to take your eye off of the ball (the ball being quality performance on the basics), then you're in trouble.

You can't win on the extras and lose on the basics and expect to survive, much less thrive.

That's Just Table Stakes

In my book, *Be the Best at What Matters Most,* I mentioned a past client that had nothing but disdain for the idea of getting better at fulfilling their customers' most basic expectations. "That's just table stakes!" they'd say.

Their perception was that they and their competitors were all very good at the basics and that the way to attracting more business (their growth was flat) was through doing "something that would set us apart."

Through some mystery shopping I did with them, I discovered that they were already setting themselves apart. Their customers were having to wait what seemed like forever to get any service at all. They were losing on the "table stakes" and didn't even realize it.

The Big Lie

Many of us are guilty of telling ourselves the big lie, which is, "We are already really good at the fundamentals." Okay, let's assume you are. My advice is to get better at those fundamentals, because that's where the game with customers is almost invariably won or lost.

The greater likelihood is that you're not as good at the basics as you think you are, because almost every business book and article we see has the message of winning "on the edges." The problem is that's not where we win or lose. We win from the "inside out," meaning that whoever wins on the core customer expectations wins it all. Beyond that, you can certainly enhance your competitive position with extras, but if you are getting beaten on any of the basics, then it's game over, and not in your favor.

Good to Great to Gone

Chelsea Bistro restaurant was a victim of complacency.

My experience in working with thousands of business owners and managers over the past 30 years tells me that there's not a lot of need to discuss the dangers of complacency in terms of everyone understanding the danger. But my experience also tells me that even though we all know that complacency kills businesses, it still remains the chief cause of business failure.

So let me simply say this: if you're thinking, "Sure, complacency is a threat to some businesses, but everything is just fine here," be afraid. Be very, very afraid, because those have been famous last words in the case of companies like Circuit City.

In his classic book *Good to Great*, Jim Collins held Circuit City up as being one of the best companies in the world and one whose practices we all should emulate. And Collins was absolutely right. Circuit City was great, until they weren't. The reason that they plummeted downhill was that they thought they had it all figured out. But, as is always the case, the "it" that they had figured out began to change in ways that they either didn't see or simply chose to ignore.

The formula for avoiding death by complacency is simple: Never stop being vigilant about how you need to change. Note that I'm not saying *if* you need to change. You do. So do I. To stay competitive and magnetic—to keep attracting new business and hang on to the business we already have—we must change. The question is always *how* to change, not *if* we should change.

- Where are making dangerous assumptions about how good we are?
- Where do we think we are already "good enough"?
- How and where are we getting complacent?
- What assumptions do we make about how good we are at the fundamentals?
- Where do we need to improve right now or risk losing our competitive edge?
- In what area are we most vulnerable at becoming complacent?

18

The Amazing, Simple, Overlooked Advantage

Stories about How Amazingly Responsive You Are

Having a consistently well-executed policy of immediate response to customers, prospects, and partners is the most overlooked and underused competitive advantage in business. It's actually difficult for me to write about this because it's so obvious, so powerful, so simple, and so available to anyone that I am in disbelief that anyone wouldn't use it.

Immediate response applies to communication with customers, prospective customers, and partners (vendors, collaborators, suppliers, etc.). It goes double, triple, or quadruple for any of those entities who are experiencing a problem. The idea is that I will respond to those people as quickly as I possibly can, or I will have a system or process in place that makes it happen automatically.

When I say automatically, I most definitely do not mean an automated, canned, one-message-for-everyone approach like, "Your e-mail/call/message is important to us. We will get back to you as quickly as we can." All that shows is that once upon a time somebody programmed an auto-response because they aren't competitive enough to give you a real response. It also says: "We're busy working on something more important than you. We'll get to you when we have some extra time. Here's a canned response to hold you off for a while."

The goal is for a real person to respond in real time in such a way that it differentiates your performance from anyone else they do business with. You want to set the standard here. You want to demonstrate that their business is the most important thing in your world. You want them telling stories to other people (prospective customers) about how amazingly responsive you are and how you don't just say that you value their business and their time, you prove it.

Brian Will Get Back to You Immediately

I was in the market for a new website designer/manager. I change my site fairly often, so it was important to me that I hire someone who responded quickly. I asked a couple of my friends whom they used and would recommend, and they both said that I should contact a guy named Brian Kraker. They both said that he did great design work and also said "he'll get back to you immediately if you have a change, problem, or question.

I hired Brian and, guess what—he truly does get back to me immediately if I have a change, problem, or question. I've since recommended him to colleagues many times.

Joe: Brian, why it is so important to you to respond quickly to customers?

Brian: I work hard on responding quickly to my customers. I've been on the other end when I've contacted customer service/support team and it takes days or even weeks before hearing anything back from them. It's a very frustrating thing. So when I started my own business, I made it my goal to respond back to my clients as soon as possible. It reminds the customer that I'm always here for them, and they appreciate that!

Joe: How do you fit in that kind of immediate response with the work that you already have on your plate every day?

Brian: During business hours I'm constantly on my computer, so I hear and see the notification whenever an e-mail is in my inbox, and I know it's there. I feel like if I don't read it, then I'm just ignoring it and it's not important to me. So I have the mind-set of "every e-mail that comes into my inbox is important to me."

Joe: How important has immediate response been in the success of your business and in continuing to build your business?

Brian: Responding quickly to e-mails has been incredibly important in the success of my business. I depend on word-of-mouth referrals. Ninety-five percent of my clients have come by word of mouth. If I'm not doing a good job with my current customers, then they wouldn't share my contact information with their friends/colleagues. I wouldn't get a continual flow of new clients, and my business would hurt from it. I rely on my clients just as much as they rely on me. So I know it's crucial to make my customers happy, and the best way I can make them happy is to always be there for my clients and respond to their e-mails and phone calls whenever they reach out to me.

A New Standard of Performance

An immediate response to customers has become such an expected standard of performance these days that I shake my head in disbelief at those who think that customers will accept anything less. Not long ago I sent an e-mail to a small company that used to provide Internet marketing services for us. The next day (already too long!) I received a reply saying that the person I was trying to contact wouldn't respond to me because he was at a business convention in Philadelphia.

What? Do they not have Internet service in Philadelphia? Is he seriously not checking e-mail for five days? If he's not, did he not make provisions for someone else to handle his customers? And if he didn't do that, did it not occur to him to send his customers advance notice that he'd be unavailable?

I fired the company.

I'm not saying that you can't have a life or that you have to be tied to your customers 24/7 without a break. But I am saying that your business has to. If you're not going to be available to respond to customers, then you've got to make alternate plans to cover it or at the very least let your customers know in advance.

I Loved Them

A big part of my job is to be on the lookout for new companies that look like they're going to be magnetic, with the potential for growth and success. I began hearing a lot about a company that delivered top-quality ingredients with recipes for great gourmet meals to your home.

I was intrigued by this whole new category of upscale meals that you cook yourself, so to get a customer's perspective, I signed up. After the first week's experience with them, I was ready to not only recommend them, but recommend them very enthusiastically. I loved them.

Here's what I wrote after that first delivery:

I don't want to go into doing a commercial so suffice it to say that these guys deliver the goods. Amazing quality food delivered fresh and on time with great recipes that are easy to follow. My daughters and I had a blast cooking together (we let Mom take a break) and I fully intend to stay with this company as a customer getting two meals delivered every Friday unless and until they give me a reason to go elsewhere.

Until I Didn't

The story took a surprising and disappointing turn, however, after my second week's experience. The food didn't show up. Delivery day (Friday) came and went. No delivery.

I called their customer service number. It turns out that on Fridays, one of the two days that they deliver meals to thousands and thousands of customers, their customer service number shuts down at 6 PM Eastern time. Having no one to speak with about my problem, I left a message. No returned call that night. I e-mailed. Nothing. No response.

Knowing this was a new company put together by smart people, I turned to what I was confident would get a response— their Facebook page. I posted about my problem and. . . . nothing. No response. Then I went for what would surely be my sure thing: Twitter. I tweeted my problem to them. Again, silence.

Now that's a "wow" factor, as in: "Wow, with the potential for delivery problems every Friday night with customers across the United States, they've all gone home."

Stunning. It was what I consider an epic fail in today's marketplace.

The love was gone.

Too Little, Too Late

Finally, the next day, I received a very nice, very professional e-mail from the company apologizing for their delivery failure. They said that they'd take that meal off my bill, and give me next week's meal free.

It was a classic case of too little, too late. Not only had they literally failed to deliver on a basic expectation (the product), but their response time was abysmal. If they had answered their phone on Friday evening or even responded reasonably quickly to my e-mail, my post on their Facebook page, or my tweets to them, it might have been a different story.

Reality check: You can't be slow to respond to customers today and expect to be competitive.

Another reality check: "Slow" means taking longer than "now."

Real-Time Response

I'm not talking about an unreasonable expectation on the part of customers. I'm simply talking about a new definition in a new customer reality. Immediate, real-time response has become the new reasonable expectation. Either meet that expectation, or lose customers to those who will.

It used to be that when all else failed in trying to reach a service or product provider, you tweeted. Now it's become the first line of communication for lots of consumers and business-to-business customers.

Entrepreneur magazine ran an article about this new customer reality:

> *"If you're not listening in social, it's like telling your call center staff to take the next month off," says Lucas Vandenberg of Fifty & Five, a digital marketing agency. "Twitter is the most real-time tool we have."*

> *Hyatt Hotels & Resorts has people working around the clock to respond in minutes to social media messaging from customers. "It's replacing calling the front desk for that subset of customers," says Dan Moriarty, director of digital strategy for Hyatt. "We don't want to pick up the phone and wait for the front desk. We want to tweet and get on with our lives."*

> *Steven Oddo, co-founder of tour company Walks of Italy, New York & Turkey, posted a tweet while in-flight requesting an earlier connection with Delta Air Lines in Atlanta. Within three minutes*

he had received a reply "I will be more than happy to place you on stand-by for that flight," and received a confirmation in less than a minute after that.

Sorry, That Won't Work for Me

I was working with a company that was proud of their 24-hour response promise to customers. I used the punchline from an old joke in telling them, "Sorry, but your 24 hour response time wouldn't work for me as a customer because of where I live." Someone finally asked, "Where do you live?"

"In the twenty-first century," I said.

Obviously, it's your call. You're certainly capable of immediate response to customers. Anyone is. If your excuse is that it costs too much money to staff for immediate response, I'll simply say that it costs you much more to not do it. If your excuse is that you're a small or even a one-person business, I'll say: "So am I. But I do it."

Immediate response to customers, prospects, and partners is something you can start doing now, as soon as you finish reading this sentence.

- If you are not responding immediately to customers, prospective customers, and business partners, why aren't you?
- What possible reason would you have for not taking advantage of this incredibly powerful and easily doable competitive advantage?

(continued)

(continued)

- If you are going to begin a strategy of immediate response, how will you make that happen?
- Who will be responsible?
- What, if any, new process do you need to establish?
- What is your schedule for implementation?
- How will you make sure that immediate response is the policy throughout your organization?

19

Tomorrow's Magnetic Business

Here are a few truths that we all need to know about the future of business and what it means to my business and yours:

The Pace of Change Will Increase

This goes into the "duh" category of what we already know, but it's vitally important to you in terms of your ability to make choices and decisions and then be able to move on to the next choices and decisions very quickly.

The speed at which changes will take place is what gives truth to the maxim "fail quickly." We have to be willing to make a decision quickly, learn from our failures, and move on to the next decision.

Here is what's going to be more challenging for you—to make a decision that succeeds and move on to the next decision instead of basking in the glow of your success. You may understand the market right now, but guess what? The market just changed. Tomorrow it will change again.

Be nimble. Be quick.

Your Customers Just Changed

You think you know your customers. Consider this:

- Your customers just got smarter. They know more about you, your product or service, and your competition than they did yesterday. It's right there on their smartphones.
- Your customers' financial situations changed this week.
- People got married. People got jobs. People graduated. How does that affect you?

- Some of your customers have talked with your competition since they last talked with you. What does that mean to you?
- Something at some business just knocked your customers' socks off. It was a business that has nothing to do with what you do, but your customer will now expect that same level of value, service, or attention from you.

If You Make Customers or Potential Customers Wait, You Lose

Period. It has become the unforgivable sin in business. Your customer used to want it now. Then they wanted it yesterday. Now they want it day before yesterday. How fast are you? How quick? Think long and hard about this one. It's a very, very big deal.

Your Customers Are Superconnected

That connection makes them superdemanding. Your support and service systems have to be at least as good as your product or initial service. Your ability to answer customer questions and resolve problems has to evolve continuously. What was considered good service six months ago will get you fired today.

Every Person in Your Organization Must Have a Customer Focus

Let's go straight to the cheesy-sounding truth: Without customers, there is no reason for any job to exist. None. Your organization must become one big customer-focused machine, and all of the parts must function together to make each customer happy.

What keeps the positive customer word-of-mouth business growth machine running is quite simply happy customers.

You Have to Change from Talking to the Market to Talking with the Market

Advertising and traditional marketing still have a place. Sometimes it's vitally important. But what's going to become more important is to have meaningful conversations with your customers. We've now got the capability to have real-time conversations with customers anywhere, any time of day. Use it. Your competition's going to.

Sell Me Stuff I Want

Years ago I was working with a group, and we had a discussion about companies that we really liked. One guy said his favorite company was Home Depot. I asked him why, and he said, "Because they sell me stuff I want." That's a good place to be—selling people stuff they want. Don't make the mistake of having to talk people into wanting what you sell. Sell them what they want. IKEA sends hundreds of their people into the homes of their customers for the express purpose of finding out how they live and what they want. Then they make it and sell it to them. Not physics.

Don't Appeal to a Demographic. Appeal to Me.

Whoever is best at marketing, selling, and communicating one on one with customers will win. Marketing to demographics is a really, really "old thinking" way to compete.

Having the Right Technology Is Great. Having the Right People Is Better.

You can't automate caring about people. No technology can make up for employees whose hearts aren't into their work and their customers. Hire the right people then give them the technology they need to make customers happy.

"Simple and Easy" Is the New Added Value

I'm a broken record about this. If you can make buying a car easier for me than another car dealer selling the exact same car, I will pay you for that added value.

If you've never thought about simplicity and ease of doing business as key elements in your value proposition, think again.

Use Video

People like little movies. They really like them a lot. Use video to tell your story, educate your employees and customers, show them how to solve problems, and sometimes use video just to have fun. Remember to keep your little movies little. Attention spans are almost nonexistent.

Win on the Basics

This is the eternal, everlasting, overriding truth: Whoever wins on the basics wins.

It's very difficult to do. You have to be really smart and really, really good. If you're not really smart and really good, then you're going to have to resort to gimmicks. (It won't work.)